New Visions
for the
Long Pastorate

Roy M. Oswald
Gail D. Hinand
William Chris Hobgood
Barton M. Lloyd

Contents

Library of Congress Catalog Card Number 83-73205
ISBN #1-56699-010-6

Prologue
A Fable

Jake has been the pastor of St. Paul's Church in the
small midwestern town of Damascus, Illinois for the
last twenty-two years. Jake is fifty-nine years
old. He feels he has had a good pastorate at St.
Paul's, but a few years ago he began to question his
future. Could he hang on at St. Paul's until retirement? The six years ahead seemed ominous. When he
thought of alternatives, he was not at all hopeful.
Jake decided that he needed to confront this issue
with some people in his congregation. He asked
twelve people to represent the congregation in dialogue on the future of his ministry with St. Paul's.
He proposed the option of their meeting by themselves
first to clarify the needs of St. Paul's.

At their joint meeting, Jake was candid. He felt
burned out and exhausted. He felt he had carried
this congregation on his shoulders and he was tired.
He was aware of this fatigue when he accounted for
time repeatedly spent with the same neurotic, dependent members of the parish. Secretly, he wished that
he could be rid of them. He was discouraged by the
prospect of continually working to raise the budget
to include enough program money to meet the congregation's goals and his salary. He wondered if he
could muster up energy for another stewardship cam-
paign. Dealing with a cantankerous organist/choir
director was getting on his nerves. He was tired of
being the general handyman around a church which
seemed to be constantly falling apart. Yet, the
thought of leaving St. Paul's was more than he could
bear. He loved these people, particularly those in

the room and those close to him. The thought of
leaving was intolerable. If he could have the best
of all worlds, he would finish out his ministry at
St. Paul's. At the same time, he was candid about
the lack of alternative prospects. It was clear that
at his age he was never going to be elected bishop.
It was also clear that he was not going to be called
to a larger parish. Making a lateral move seemed
idiotic. Considering these alternatives, he much
preferred staying at St. Paul's. He was ready to
hear the committee's candid feedback of their sense
of what another six years with him would be like.

The committee had met ahead of time and was prepared for this. For years they had watched Jake
grind himself into the ground. His pot belly and his
overweight condition were an irritation to them.
They did not feel his marriage was much of a model
for the parish. They wished the nature of that relationship, which they sensed suffered from his failure
to spend quality time at home, was better. They
admitted they did not feel he was either a dynamic
preacher or a good administrator. His strongest suit
was as a counselor. Over the last few years he had
become lax. He did not press for innovation and new
ideas as he had in the past. He wasn't paying attention to the concerns and needs of the people around
him. They felt that for the most part he had been
coasting for the last two years. On the other hand,
they loved him dearly and could not tolerate the
thought of his leaving. He had seen them through
many crises and turmoil—each one of them—and they
wanted him there as their resident holy man. They
would like him to stay until retirement, but some
things would need to change for that to be productive
for both the congregation and Jake. The meeting
ended with both Jake and the group agreeing to think
more about what would be the nature of the contract
that would satisfy both parties if Jake were to stay
until retirement at age sixty-five. The committee
agreed to gather data from other parishioners; Jake
agreed to explore ways to deal with the feedback he
had been given.

Jake was stunned by the feelings they expressed.
At home he spent the rest of the afternoon and
evening talking with his wife Betty about what had
taken place. It was the first serious conversation
he had had with her in months. He was shocked by his
own candor, but even more shocked by the candor of
this group of laity. It was true that he had been
sliding lately, but he wasn't aware this was obvious. He wondered if he was up to meeting their
expectations of him if he were to continue at St.
Paul's. Betty encouraged Jake to return to therapy
with his old friend Tom Carruthers, whom he had not
seen for years. If he were to go through this evaluation process, he needed a broader base of support.

A month later the group met once again with Jake
to work out a plan for his staying. The first thing
agreed upon was that Jake needed to go on sabbatical,
to get away, to get hold of his life, and to develop
new sources of energy and vision for himself and the
parish. The group recommended that Jake get training
in managing stress and avoiding burnout and begin to
monitor himself more faithfully regarding self-care.
They also hoped he and Betty would engage in a marriage enrichment seminar. In addition, the committee
asked that prior to Jake's sabbatical, an evaluation,
using input from a random sample of the parish, be set
up to ascertain areas of ministry that needed attention and support.

Jake had a few requests of his own. He asked that
a personnel committee be set up to help him manage
the parish staff, particularly to help him deal with
the parish organist. He also asked that this committee consider hiring a part-time parish administrator. In particular, he wanted the administrator's
first two priorities to be working with the stewardship committee and the property committee.

The committee indicated its willingness to explore
Jake's requests with the church council. Jake said
he was ready to give all their requests serious
consideration. He requested an outside facilitator
to manage parish and pastoral evaluation. He was in
agreement with the proposal for a six month sabbati-

cal. During that time he would be willing to take
both a seminar on preaching and a marriage enrichment
seminar with Betty. He also agreed that he could use
some training related to self-care, stress and burnout.

Several months later, the group met once again.
The parish survey had been completed with the help of
an outside consultant. One thing that became clear
was that parishioners really wanted Jake to work less
hard and to concentrate more on his own spiritual
life. They needed and wanted someone who was less
frantic and had more spiritual depth. In addition,
they wanted Jake to decrease his control over certain
programs and to turn leadership over to lay groups.
Last, they wanted him to continue the kind of love
and care he had been giving them over the years. The
evaluation pointed to Jake's conflict avoidance style
and its long-term negative effects on the parish.
Jake agreed to add attendance at a conflict management seminar to gain skills in dealing with parish
problems to the list of things to do on his sabbatical.

The committee met one more time with Jake, just
prior to his leaving on sabbatical, as a final check
to see if both were still in agreement. The tone of
that meeting was definitely upbeat. Both Jake and
the group were surprised at how far they had come
since their initial meeting months before. One item
was added to the overall plan. Jake agreed to lead
the congregation in a goal-setting process which
would help both himself and the congregation target
things they wanted to see happen in the parish in the
next six years until his retirement.

That evening a huge party was held for Jake and
Betty. There was a real sense of joy and celebration
over the work they had accomplished and had agreed to
do together. The congregation had negotiated a
healthy new relationship with its religious authority. It all seemed very workable. Both the parish
and Jake and Betty felt like winners. It was clear
that Jake was going to give this effort his best
shot. Neither Jake nor the parish had given up on

each other, allowing a deteriorating, demoralizing situation to drag on during his remaining six years of ministry. Following the party, the bishop, who was present, conducted a service of recommitment. So ends the fable.

The story of Jake and Betty is a fable because in reality issues are never quite that clear and simple. It is rare for such a high level of candor and openness to exist between pastor and people, allowing problems to be worked through so quickly and easily. A committee of twelve rarely represents the wishes and opinions of an entire parish so clearly. Normally, a parish is more divided into pro and con pastor factions. Finally, it is unlikely that areas of discontent between pastor and parishioners can be so easily identified and dealt with so successfully.

The unreality of this fable demonstrates the need for our study on the long pastorate, and for the development of theories, designs and recommendations on this issue.

Introduction:
Methodology and Process

The Alban Institute study of long pastorates began
March 19-20, 1979 in Framingham, Massachusetts. Four
judicatories (three regional and one national) participated: three Episcopal dioceses in the northeast
(Connecticut, Maine, and Massachusetts) and the Unitarian Universalist Association. Twelve judicatory
representatives gathered for these two days to:

Determine what was already known about long
pastorates;
Develop assumptions that needed to be tested;
Agree on procedures and costs.

From October 1-4, 1979, twenty-eight clergy and
spouses (seven Unitarian Universalist and twenty-one
Episcopalian) gathered for Part I of the first Long
Pastorate Seminar. They were debriefed on issues
related to long pastorates, exploring what had
happened in their own long pastorates. They then
entered a research phase, a three month period
gathering data in their home parishes before re-
turning for Part II. The same group met January
14-17, 1980, for further sharing and study.

This three-phase process was repeated in two other
locations at two different times. Twenty North and
South Carolina and Virginia clergy and their spouses,
representing Lutherans, Presbyterians and Episcopal-
ians, met during 1981. In New England, another study
was conducted involving only Episcopal clergy and
their spouses. There were eighteen participants in
that study. A total of thirty-three clergy and
twenty-nine spouses participated in this research.

Spouse attendance was strongly encouraged in all
three studies. Twenty-nine out of a possible thirty-
three participated; four clergy were single. The
clergy ranged from thirty-eight to sixty years in
age; the spouses from thirty to fifty-eight.

Five instruments were used in the study:

Pre-conference Data Gatherer (Oswald, Hobgood,
Lloyd, 1979);
Myers-Briggs Type Indicator (Myers and Briggs,
1976);
Pastor/Parish Fit (Oswald, 1980);
Clergy Burnout Inventory (Oswald, 1982);
Laity Questionnaire (Oswald, 1979).

Action research methodology was utilized which allowed the research team to gather primary data from
participants while at the same time developing seminar designs that facilitated the growth and awareness
of the participants.

The title, "New Visions for a Long Pastorate,"
originated from our discovery of powerful evidence
favoring long pastorates. It is a vision that
emerged despite our own initial negative assumptions about such pastorates. The four researchers
all changed their minds on this issue after the eight
days with clergy and their spouses. In fact, we have
come to see that:

While all the disadvantages of a long pastorate
can be managed with skill and training, few of
the enormous advantages of a long pastorate are
available to shorter ministries.

This report is our attempt to outline the chief
disadvantages of a long pastorate, ways to overcome
them, and the special advantages. Our aim is to help
clergy and spouses in long pastorates capitalize more
effectively on what we have learned. The areas we
discuss are:

Summary of Research Findings

Our major learnings about the risk and promise of
the long pastorate indicate, as our prologue
suggests, some clear advantages. All of us are
aware, however, of the many long pastorates that
are stale and lifeless at best, and downright
disgraceful to the Christian Church at worst.
Those who risk long tenure in a pastorate need to
know the price of failure. Though the stakes are
high, the advantages clearly indicate that for
alert, competent clergy, the risks are worth
taking.

The Gap Theory

Probably our most profound discovery has been the
Gap Theory. It highlights a major challenge to be
faced in every effective long pastorate.

Support Pillars of Healthy Long Pastorates

If church officials, clergy and their congregations pay attention to these five dimensions of
long pastorates, it is our belief they will have
the greatest chance for a healthy, vibrant
pastorate.

Spouses in Long Pastorates

Our survey indicates various ways in which spouses
have approached this role.

The Pastor/Parish Fit

The instrument we used in this study to help evaluate present compatibility between pastor and
parish is self scoring, and may be useful to the
reader.

Reflections

Long pastorates are as different as the people in
them. We have come to see them as a continuum
between those which are solid and healthy with
many reasons for continuance, to those which have
obviously run their course and should be termin-
ated. Even when talented, dedicated people are

involved, circumstances--either internal or
external--often make a continuing relationship
unwise. Seven profiles which exemplify clergy in
long pastorates are included in the report.
Names and places have been changed for privacy.
These profiles were chosen to illustrate the wide
spectrum in long pastorates.

  We are pleased you have taken an interest in this
study and our findings. You can join us in the real-
ization that some of our clergy in long pastorates
are the unsung heroes of the church.

I. Stories of Long Pastorates

Clergy

Clifford Freed

Clifford has been the minister at Greensburg Church for twenty-three years. The church had sixty members when he began; now the membership hovers around 300 and the facilities are used to capacity at all times for congregational and community activities.

Clifford is ideally suited both for this parish and for a long pastorate. He is loved and respected by the membership. He is a pastor continually involved in the spiritual journey of his people. In his words: "The longer I stay in this place, the more I see. I continue to be fascinated with the revelation of new life going on right in our midst and the steady unfolding of people with whom I work. New possibilities seem to open up for me on a regular basis in my current scene."

However, Clifford needed some help in dealing with the stigma he felt others placed on his pastorate. In his denomination, few people stay twenty-three years. He felt pressure from his colleagues in ministry to move. Clifford also needed assistance in facing some key issues if he were to remain with this parish. He and his wife had just separated. They had been a real team in this ministry. Could he manage without her? The seminar was able to give the help Clifford sought.

Clifford now plans to stay at Greensburg Church for at least another five years. That decision became clear to him as he had the opportunity during both phases of the seminar and in the interim period to critique thoroughly his long pastorate. He and his parish can continue to have a love affair that never seems to lose its charm and energy and that continues to spur both into living up to their greatest potential.

Ken Ristine

Ken has been pastor of the liberal First Church for eleven years. He has always wanted to exercise his ministry in an urban setting, and this situation in a southern city has been ideal. The congregation of over 300 members has had a consistent 150 worshippers throughout these eleven years.

Initially, Ken had some rough times of interpersonal tension with the bookkeeper/secretary and with the janitor/musician. Both were let go when it became clear a harmonious working relationship could never develop. Once that tension was resolved, Ken's ministry took hold and has remained effective through the years.

Ken's high credibility and level of trust with congregation members has enabled him to guide the church in facing some tough issues. The Vietnam controversy brought much stress, but the congregation stayed intact. In the early '70s the church building was used by a group counseling enlisted personnel from a nearby army base. Later, the request of a gay community to use the facilities for worship brought forth the most difficult decision ever faced by the church; again, the congregation remained intact and the request was granted.

Ken has given the congregation sound prophetic preaching within a continually changing worship format. He has kept himself alert and alive through frequent continuing education and regular sabbaticals. Ken and his wife June are much beloved by the congregation, who have followed their four boys into and through adolescence. Although husband and wife are strongly committed to each other, their marriage has suffered some neglect because of Ken's heavy

involvement with the church. With two boys still at
home, their life style needs to be revised to allow
more time together as a family.

Ken and June came to the seminar with many questions. Were they too complacent in this comfortable
ministry? Would staying another few years adversely
affect Ken's church career? What would be the
effects on their marriage, family patterns, and
June's position as a teacher in the public schools?
The seminar helped Ken and June clarify these issues
and affirm their current ministry. They clearly
wanted to continue in ministry, and Ken could not
envision another situation that would provide him a
comparable opportunity at this time.

With their decision to stay for at least another
five years came the need to focus on a new vision and
thrust toward the future. Specific items needed to
be negotiated with the congregation. Together Ken
and June needed to make commitments to work on their
marriage and strengthen their family life. Ken
needed to be clear about the learning experiences he
wants and to plan concretely his continuing education
in the next five years in order to keep himself
alive, fresh, and growing in this congregation.

Bernard Otto

St. John's Parish and Bernard Otto had been wedded
for fifteen years when he attended The Alban Institute's Long-Tenured Pastorate Seminar. When Bernie
first began working with us, he was ambivalent about
whether he should stay or move. He had enjoyed a
fine pastorate at St. John's; through the years at
the parish, a healthy tension had existed between him
and the congregation. In the '60s, when race and
Vietnam tore at most congregations, Bernie was able
to help his stay together while, at the same time,
holding their feet to the fire on the issues. There
would be much pain in leaving St. John's. By the end
of the seminars it had become clear to Bernie that he
had to leave. He had been fooling himself about his
parish. The truth was that he no longer had the

energy or the commitment to take them deeper. He had
been coasting for the last five years. He needed a
new challenge to keep his own growing edge alive. As
an attractive, talented pastor, he would move easily.

Ron Swift

Ron Swift's distress was obvious from the start. Ron
was stuck. He had been with Grace Church for twenty-
four years. He had tried to move several times, but
always got turned down near the end of each search
process. Depressed and demoralized, he stopped
looking for a few years and then tried again. His
anger was deeply buried, but it would emerge inap-
propriately within the parish. The consequences left
him even more depressed. The two week-long seminars
helped him put together a plan of action that would
move him within a year—one that would work because
not only was it strategically sound, it also had
enough built-in support to sustain him and his wife
through the job hunting process.

Michael Peters

Michael Peters couldn't make up his mind. He just
flat-out, absolutely couldn't make up his mind! He
and Jodie moved to Wanksville eighteen years ago when
he was called to be associate minister of Old Central
Church. When the senior pastor retired, Michael,
after an interim period, was asked to remain and head
the church. That was twelve years ago.

Jodie has been very much a part of his ministry at
Old Central. She and Michael frequently make calls
together and, with Michael's blessing and after
thorough discussion between the two of them, she
often tackles some of the congregation's touchiest
interpersonal problems. They are truly together in
marriage and ministry; the only place they part
company is when they discuss leaving for another
ministry. Jodie is at home in Wanksville, the community where they have lived for most of their
married life and where their children were born,

educated, and loved. Michael, while happy in his
work, is less wedded to the idea of staying forever.

The ministry has been very good for Old Central
Church. Michael initiated bylaw changes resulting in
more effective decision making and internal management. The congregation became more responsible about
investments, mission and evangelism. From being a
rather narrow, isolated, exclusive club, Old Central
has become an open and caring community. Members'
skills are well utilized, as in persuading local
industrial officials to apply their knowledge to
church issues. Community service is strongly
emphasized; music and the arts are encouraged and
celebrated; and the congregation has become active
in inviting new people to share in its life.

However, Michael is confronting a deadline. While
Old Central is healthy and his family is happy in
Wanksville, Michael is at an age which necessitates a
decision to stay or leave within the next few years.
He's discovered that it isn't enough to congratulate
himself on how well things are going. Nor is it
enough to decide merely to put his name in circula-
tion for a new parish and see what happens. Before
he does anything, or nothing, he has to make up his
mind!

James Jacquitt

James is ready to move! He has been with the Flatlands Church for fifteen years. When he arrived, it
was a small congregation, very dependent on its
regional church office for financial and pastoral
help. James was chosen by the denomination to help
get Flatlands on its feet.

Several factors have hindered this. Because of
its remote location, Flatlands Church has had difficulty getting leadership training and other assistance needed to do the "growing up" imperative for its
growth. The Flatlands community, a small industrial
and college town, has a high population turnover.
The Flatlands Church has had a ninety-five percent
turnover since James became pastor! Developing a

strong, consistent membership has been nearly impossible.

Early in his pastorate James was called upon by the denomination to direct a summer camp. He later became caught between pressure from the local church to give up the camp work and from the denomination to continue as camp director. He now says that he did not deal well with the ensuing stress, developing emotional problems and increased alcohol dependence.

About seven years into this pastorate, James said, a new member "tried to separate me from the parishioners" with false accusations. James outlasted her and his relationship with the congregation deepened. Two years ago, however, he had another severe personal and emotional crisis. Following treatment, James is feeling better than he has in years. His marriage has gained new strength. His spouse Betty speaks of a rich life together, one that has allowed both fulfillment and space to find new spiritual depths. Their youngest child will graduate from high school soon. They both feel it is time to take serious steps towards a new ministry.

And so, they face a new crisis of sorts. How will they make this move? Should James remain in parish ministry or enter the counseling field, where he can blend his skills and his personal experiences to do ministry in another arena? The seminar came at the right time for him to face these options and to make some decisions.

Herb Sanders

Herb and his wife Sally would like to stay in their parish of 325 communicants in a lovely New England town, but have some doubts. Herb has served sixteen years in this parish, his first solo pastorate out of seminary. In those sixteen years, the congregation has not grown appreciably, even though the annual budget has doubled. His nagging question is: would this parish grow numerically under other pastoral leadership?

Herb and Sally see many fruits of their labors,

however, other than numbers. Their congregation was heavily involved in the racial turmoil of the '60s. During an anti-Semitic controversy in the town over ten years ago, their parish began dialogue seminars with a nearby Jewish congregation which have continued to the present. In 1973, their governing board endorsed the lettuce boycott, then the grape boycott in 1974. In 1975, the parish sponsored several Vietnamese families, and most recently the parish held a Human Sexuality workshop attended by forty people. Herb feels very trusted by his parish, yet also taken for granted.

Another of Herb's concerns and doubts has to do with his midlife status. At forty-six, what would happen if he stayed five years? What are his chances of being called elsewhere at age fifty-one? His professional development is another concern. Is this parish like an old shoe that no longer stretches? Are there new challenges for him? And, finally, both Herb and Sally are aware of a few people in the parish who really would like to see them move. Are these the vocal minority present in most parishes, or are they the visionaries who see more clearly the potential of the parish under new pastoral leadership?

By the seminar's end, the two had decided to stay, and they felt good about the decision. Through some solid data gathering in their parish during the interim between phase I and II, they discovered the congregation was basically healthy and receiving good pastoral care under Herb's leadership. Herb then became more confident his ministry could grow and develop in that place for a while longer, and he and Sally returned home renewed and revitalized by their experience.

Observations About Pastors

Statistics reveal that within large major Protestant denominations clergy are remaining longer in the same local church than during the period from the 1940s through the 1970s. A variety of factors contributes to this:

The professional career path of clergy spouses as more clergy spouses enter professions which do not invite mobility;

Home ownership by clergy as it has become the norm for clergy to purchase their own homes rather than to live in church-owned property;

Overabundance of clergy in most "mainline" denomnations as the job market for clergy has tightened up, making less opportunity for mobility;

Sabbatical leaves in which renewal is gained through study rather than in a move;

Leveling of salary, with smaller differences in salaries between large and small churches;

Increased mobility of North Americans, with the result that congregations are in transition while clergy offer stability.

These factors stimulated researchers to ask several questions. Are these phenomena healthy for clergy, their families and their congregations? What are long pastorates, beyond an arbitrary designation of more than ten years in the same local church? What myths and prejudices are held about long pastorates? Why do some long pastorates remain vital and alive, while others deteriorate over time? What do clergy and congregations need to do to keep long pastorates mutually beneficial? What, if any, help is being offered clergy who may find themselves ambivalent about remaining in parishes? How can clergy who want to move be helped to do so? Examination of these questions provided information useful for denominations and their executives, local churches and their leaders, and clergy and their families.

Spouses

One clear message we received in all three of our
Long-tenured Pastorate Seminars was gratitude that
spouses were included in this study.

One of the spouses shared this perception:

In all the years I have been a pastor's wife in
the church, this is the first event I was ever
invited to outside my congregation where my input
was taken seriously and my contribution valued.

From the beginning, we felt it would be
inappropriate to ask clergy to examine their long
pastorates without including their spouses. Whether
the decision is to stay or leave, the spouse needs to
be an integral part of that decision. In retrospect,
the inclusion of spouses was one of the more astute
judgments we made.

The Long-tenured Pastorate Study gave us a glimpse
at the lives of twenty-nine women married to clergy
in long pastorates. While this is by no means a
sample to satisfy an exacting researcher, common
experiences of this distinctive group emerged.

William Douglas' 1965 comprehensive study, Ministers' Wives,[1] based on 5,000 clergy spouse descrip-
tions of their involvement, activity patterns and
degree of role satisfaction, led him to identify
three classifications: the teamworker, the back-
ground supporter and the detached spouse. More re-
cent studies, reflecting changing times, added a
fourth type--the career woman.

These are valid in classifying wives of long-
tenured clergy. Of course, these women were unique
individuals in their own right. They did not fit any
outworn stereotype of the "parson's wife." They were
helpmates and supporters, yes, and sometimes suffer-
ing servants and passive appendages. They have characterized their role as a job and a burden; they have
been resentful; they have been in love with it all.
Some run the show; some have never found their place;

some are burned out; some have very independently
forged their own lives. Whether for economic reasons
or for personal fulfillment, almost all are employed
for pay, at least part time, outside the home and
parish.

With only a few sad exceptions, these twenty-nine
women have made peace in positive ways with their
role as a minister's wife. Long tenure in one place
has allowed them to work through the "should/have to"
syndrome, whether imposed by husband, congregation or
self, and the end result is a clearer self-identity.

Statistically, twenty were Episcopalian, four were
members of the Presbyterian Church in the United
States, three were Unitarian Universalist, and two
were members of the Lutheran Church in America.
Twenty-eight were mothers and several were grand-
mothers. One, an Episcopal priest and psychologist,
married a long-tenured pastor five years ago and they
have no children. Twenty-eight women resided on the
eastern seaboard from Maine to North Carolina; one
lived in Kentucky.

They were remarkably open, trusting and willing to
share their experiences freely. Their overall emotional health (sense of identity, how they saw themselves as clergy wives and general satisfaction with
their lives) appeared very good to excellent with
only one or two exceptions. The stability of their
living situations had contributed to this in a positive rather than negative way. They had settled in
one place for a long time; they were comfortable in
knowing and being known by the parishioners; they
could respond to what seemed to be expected of them;
they were familiar with, and to, the community; their
children had grown up in one place and also "felt"
the community. Having an established place of their
own, they valued being seen as separate from their
husbands.

Of course, not all was positive. Most of their
frustrations and concerns had to do with a need for
more time, with never ending demands, with housing
woes, of how to be more supportive to their husbands
as they struggled together over whether to stay or

leave and, frankly, with fatigue from repeatedly coping with the same people with the same problems.

Following are brief glimpses of some of these long-tenured clergy spouses. (Names and identifying details have been altered.)

Teamworkers

Louise Nickerson

The teamwork of Louise and Paul sounds delightful. Both share a high commitment to their small inner city parish and to long-term goals consistent with an inclusive and ecumenical religious community. Their "we" means strategizing and sharing together, while acknowledging and supporting each other's particular gifts.

Louise seems truly at peace with her role. She talks of her future in this place as continuing to do more, to do it even better and to expand on the fine ministry that has been carried out thus far. She speaks distinctly of her skills and contributions and foresees further schooling in a helping profession to equip her even more. One senses in Louise a very high level of activity, satisfaction and sense of call to their ministry in a way that demonstrates a positive helpmate role. Louise seems to be a clergy wife with a stable, organized value system expressed in a totally integrated way of life--calm, helpful and composed, yet very involved, committed and adequate to the task.

Julie Goodman

In contrast, listening to Julie is like listening to a supermom, Pollyanna and assistant rector all rolled into one, with the editorial "we" thrown in for emphasis. It's difficult to separate Julie and who she is from Jerry, her rector spouse, and impossible to separate her from his ministry. She responds to questions for him, answers in the plural and writes as though she was the pastor. With pride and a sense of "rightness," Julie describes "their" ministry as a partnership and her part as having coffee with those who are having problems, doing an enormous amount of phoning, having many meetings and meals at the rectory, making parish calls with Jerry, providing overnight sheltering for problem parishioners, etc.

While the attributes she values in a clergy wife—nurturing, mothering, hugging, consoling, opening up the community—sound very helpful, in fact her style seems controlling. While quick to affirm Jerry's strengths and to acknowledge that he is really in charge, her words and actions often belie these words. Furthermore, in her rational, practical manner she will not so subtly remind Jerry that their job is still where they are, thus heightening his ambivalence about moving. The "Siamese twins" aspect of this couple seems stifling. Unfortunately, Julie seems to epitomize the less healthy teamworker role.

Background Supporters

Norene Renton

Norene is a supporter who sees her role as positive—yet who has some doubts. She is warm, open, attractive, with a sense of humor and demeanor that makes one aware of how comfortable she is with herself. Her attributes include being supportive and friendly and having a genuine liking for people. But, Norene has been struggling with her supportive role and is beginning to move toward decisions that may affect her availability to the parish. Having chosen to remain a volunteer rather than being employed, she has become very involved in parish life and work. She often fills in for her husband Ralph when parish emergencies arise; when Ralph is overwhelmed with work, she does some additional "rescuing" as well. One senses she really does like to help and has not done these things in a grudging way; however, at times she has felt "used" and by now has reached her

limit of always being available and helpful to
others.

Norene finds Ralph dependent upon her in ways she
doesn't always appreciate. She fears she protects
him too much when some of his inadequacies are revealed or when she worries about the future. She
feels guilty in not wanting to continue this helper/
supporter role, but she's tired of being Ralph's
backup support all the time. Norene seems to need
permission to work through the guilty feeling and to
get on with being herself with lessened pressure to
make choices about where she puts her considerable
energies. Perhaps she would then find a redefined,
more comfortable, more detached role for herself.

Pat Dodson

Pat identifies her spouse Jim as an empathetic, able
and effective preacher. She describes herself as a
loyal, caring idea producer and long-term planner.
She supports Jim, no matter what; she feeds ideas to
him; she performs countless backup and at home functions which allow Jim to put his job first. Pat
works hard to serve and help manage his ministry; she
is hurt when this support is not acknowledged, affirmed or encouraged, especially by Jim. Jim picks
and chooses from ideas she proposes, readings she
marks for him, her observations on how he's being
treated and her analysis of parishioners. The pas-
sive/aggressive style Jim displays puzzles and angers
Pat.

Pat seems angry at others as well—those who seem
to be undercutting Jim's effectiveness as senior pastor, those who are urging him to move and those who
confront them and the style they project as a couple. Management skills like Pat's could be helpful
to a clergy husband, especially if he lacks those
particular skills and if that role is wanted and
valued by him. But the benefits can be outweighed by
side effects and fallout which, in Pat's case, seem
to have occurred.

Detached Spouses

Betty Parsons

A sharp, efficient, self-sufficient woman with training in a helping profession, Betty is very clear
about being in a stage of her life where she is ready
to move on to whatever may come.

She acknowledges she is a "pond person" who de-
sires community "roots" for herself and her family.
The small, rather remote New England town where the
parish is located is good for Betty--townspeople
recognize her, she's able to work part time at something she likes and the schools are excellent.

Betty also recognizes she is very different
from when she first moved with her husband to serve
this church. Her identity as the pastor's wife is
not as tied to the "oughts" or "shoulds" as it once
was, and she knows that in a new situation she will
not slip back into the old mode, but will carry out
the functions of a clergy wife because she wishes to
do so. She is moving toward greater detachment on
principle--not out of anger or rebellion.

The last several years have been rough for her
husband and he's now ready to move. In turn, Betty
has been retreating from people, cutting down on her
outside involvements and spending time reevaluating
her situation and their life. This reflection has
brought about a renewal, an energizing readiness to
move, psychologically and physically. She envisions
getting further skills training to enlarge her vocational focus.

Betty sees the closeness of her marriage moving
from concern/dependency to greater balance where
together she and her spouse can make decisions with
positive effects. The time seems right for Betty,
filled with excitement and a sense of adventure, to
move.

June Lawson

June, on the other hand, comes across as a narcis-

sistic, angry woman whose detachment from all but the
most social aspects of her husband's ministry seems
to come from some unclear intense rebellion. One
gains no sense of how she perceives her "role," as
she never speaks about it; rather, her life appears
to be almost totally caught up in tennis and country
club activities in her affluent community. Tragic-
ally, her dependence upon and substantial abuse of
both alcohol and tobacco has adverse effects as well,
and it is hard to differentiate cause from effect.
She is clearly resentful of her husband's passivity;
he is a likeable, open, reasonably intelligent fellow
who has been very comfortable and successful in the
same parish for many years. June seems to resent any
action on his part that might alter their current
situation. Her nagging style doesn't contribute to
the well-being of their marriage--nor does his "nice-
guy" response. This pattern, an unfortunate "game,"
is very atypical of the clergy couples in the study.
Detachment with rebellion is neither an attractive
nor a common role for clergy wives, but this is one
example.

Career Women

We see this as the clergy spouse role of the future
for many reasons: economics, changing perceptions of
the role of the "pastor's wife" and changes in the
lives of all women. Many seminar participant wives
were employed as full-time teachers, librarians, sec-
retaries, health care providers, or in other careers
or professions. Two have moved into this responsibility fairly recently as their family and parish
responsibilities were lightened by choice or design.

Sue Culp

Sue appears to have made the transition from back-
ground supporter to career woman with relative ease.
Her feminism is evident as she challenges assumptions
about what is expected of clergy wives as opposed to
other wives and/or why that should differ from what

is expected of her husband relative to her professional position at a university. She is very clear that she does not wish to share or participate in his ministry any more than he wishes to share or participate in her job. Acknowledging the double standard of the ministry, however, she admits she shares more in the life of the church than he does in the university. It appears that such involvement might come from their long tenure, with her earlier, more prescribed, pre-career role as the clergy wife.

Ann Watson

Ann has moved from full time teamworker to supporter as the time demands of her career increased and her children went away to school She did not yield the teamworker role easily, however, and continues to be quite directive of her spouse Ted. The unresolved tension is evident. She both demands equal recognition of her developing career and its importance in any decision on moving and yet acknowledges and pushes Ted's career advancement aims, sometimes even more than he does. The intensity with which she approaches everything can be overwhelming and frightening and raises questions about the residue of anger behind those demands.

Eileen Hanson

Eileen, a third career woman clergy spouse, married Ken five years ago after he had been serving his parish for five years. Eileen is an autonomous woman with an independent career, whose present position surpasses Ken's in both income and status. Parishioners viewed her from the beginning as a professional married to their rector.

Ken is presently burned out and needs to move or be rejuvenated. Both Eileen and Ken are clear about each other's career needs and the possible struggles they may involve. Their over-solicitous accommodation of each other, as in many relatively healthy dual career marriages, is made no less easy by the

overlay of church norms. Eileen, a very warm, gra-
cious, accepting woman, speaks with pleasure of her
role in the parish as Ken's wife, while clearly
neither defining nor carrying out that role in a
traditional way.

II. Research Findings
Promise and Risk in a Long Pastorate

When the study of long pastorates was first con-
ceived, our research team tended to feel that the
disadvantages of long pastorates outweighed, if they
did not eclipse, the advantages. Those of us working
in career centers were very familiar with pastors who
had "overstayed" their tenure--pastors who felt stuck
and locked in by the glutted job market, pastors who
found themselves frequently at odds with parishioners
who wished they would move. These clergy usually
manifested a mixture of burnout, discouragement and
declining self-confidence--emotional and spiritual
shackles which stifle healthy initiatives, both in
the exercise of ministry and the implementation of a
move to another parish. We expected to find a pre-
dominance of such clergy in our study.

That expectation was reinforced by denominational
executives who expressed a desperate need for help
with such burned out, "stuck" clergy, and for resources to help "unstick" them.

Adding to our negative bias toward lengthy pastorates was an unexamined assumption[2] that most long
pastorates reflected some defect in the pastor. A
widely current norm in many denominations is for a
pastor to stay in a given church for at least five
years but no longer than ten years. That norm is
reinforced by the widespread cultural notion that to
advance you need to move (a notion that begs the
question of what "to advance" means in the ordained
ministry). Participants in the Long-tenured Pastorate Study, all of whom had remained in their parishes
over ten years (some over twenty years), testified

that both fellow clergy and denominational leaders
felt "something was wrong" with them because they had
not moved more frequently.

We were surprised and impressed early in the study
that the majority of the participants were in what
appeared to be healthy long pastorates. Thus, the
potential and promise of a long pastorate surfaced
immediately. It is possible that our sample of
clergy was skewed. We knew some troubled long-
tenured clergy had not responded to the invitation to
take part in the study. Two or three who had ac-
cepted cancelled at the last minute. Our sample may
overrepresent the healthy end of the spectrum. If
so, it points to the possibilities even for those at
the other end. The participants formed a good group
from which to learn firsthand both the advantages and
benefits of long pastorates, and some of the disadvantages.

Four primary sources were used to gather data on
the advantages and disadvantages:

Denominational leaders and executives;
Long-tenured pastors;
Their spouses;
Lay people from their parishes.

Approaches to these groups varied.
Denominational leaders were first asked to gather
information through telephone calls to long-tenured
pastors and were then asked, in a conference setting,
to brainstorm potential advantages and disadvantages
of long pastorates.

At the beginning of their first conference, participating clergy and their spouses were asked to
brainstorm on the advantages and disadvantages of
long pastorates which they themselves had experienced.

Lay people (eight per clergy) were approached
through written questionnaires distibuted to them by
the participating clergy between the two conference
sessions in which the clergy took part.

Despite these varied methods of data gathering,
there was a striking consensus among the groups on

both the potential advantages and disadvantages of long pastorates. From the pastors, as well as their spouses, a clear sense that the advantages outweighed the disadvantages emerged. (The selection of participants may well have been an influencing factor.)

Since the largest sample surveyed was the laity, who responded to a written questionnaire, the largest volume of data came from that source. Laity were asked two questions:

From your perspective what are the six main advantages of a long pastorate (ten years or more)?

What are the six main disadvantages?

Key Findings

The seminars produced a wealth of data about the Long-tenured Pastorate (LTP). Overall, the data reversed previous negative assumptions and verified the possibility of healthy, growing LTPs for both clergy and congregations.

There was remarkable similarity among the separate groups in the identification of the advantages and disadvantages of a LTP. LTP advantages were categorized by the researchers into the following six findings:

A LTP makes possible greater in-depth knowledge of and relationships between the pastor and individual church members as well as between clergy and the congregation as a whole;

Experiencing a LTP makes possible cumulative developing knowledge and experience of each other for both clergy and congregation, as they observe and participate in each other's growth over time;

Greater continuity and stability of leadership and program in a LTP makes possible events not possible during a short tenure;

A LTP opens up possibilities of greater personal and spiritual growth for both clergy and congregation;

A LTP makes possible deeper knowledge of and participation by the clergy in the community (local, professional, ecumenical, larger denominational); and

A LTP allows additional personal benefits for both the clergy and his/her family.

Eight potential disadvantages were found:

A LTP may lead to overidentification between the clergy and congregation;

In a LTP, a gap may develop between the clergy and a growing number of the congregation;

In a LTP, there is danger that a stagnant, ineffective climate can develop;

In a LTP, there is a greater danger of clergy burnout;

As negative influences of a LTP mount and begin to outweigh positive influences, a downward spiral may develop;

An unhealthy LTP can ultimately lead both clergy and congregation to feel they are helplessly stuck with each other;

A LTP may produce reduced personal benefits for the clergy and their families.

Potential Advantages of a Long Pastorate

It should be clarified that our references to the "advantages" and "disadvantages" of long pastorates

are really to <u>potential</u> advantages and <u>potential</u>
disadvantages. There is no guarantee that either
will necessarily occur. Hence our preceding sub-
title: "Promise and Risk in a Long Pastorate."

The advantages can be categorized in a variety of
ways. In the following, advantages are in order of
frequency of occurrence. Sample responses are
included under each category.

1. A long pastorate makes possible deeper knowledge and relationships between pastor, parishioners
and the parish as a whole.

Good knowledge of the families in the parish and
the ups and downs in their lives.

Increased knowledge of the parish unit--spiritual-
ly and operationally.

Time to get acquainted with "all sorts and condi-
tions" within a parish.

Trust of parishioners.

Parishioners [who] may be more open with a minister they've known a long time

Feeling of [the pastor] truly belonging as part of
the church family instead of [being a] "visiting
relative."

2. A long pastorate makes possible cumulative
developing knowledge and experience of each other as
both pastor and parish see and participate in each
other's growth over time.

[Opportunity to] accumulate shared memories with
each other.

Better rapport with the [parish] children as
[pastor] is able to watch them develop through
church school and youth groups.

Opportunity to grow and change together, in each other's presence, and to encourage and help each other to live...[a] kind of relationship [that] takes time, years, to develop and live out.

[Opportunity to be] more effective as a pastor and counselor because of the...knowledge stemming from shared experiences.

[Opportunity for] pastor...to know talents of more people for greater involvement of lay people.

Parishioners [who] get to see more than just the novice pastor...the maturing leader.

3. There is greater continuity and stability of leadership and program in a long-term pastorate, which makes possible things which are not possible in a short-term pastorate.

[Opportunity] to follow long-term projects to completion.

[Time for] pastor and parish...to make long-range plans.

[One] of the few remaining symbols of stability.

Opportunity to develop ministries with longer time horizons.

Staff [which] does not have to keep getting used to a new minister.

Parish [which is] not constantly torn by different leadership styles.

Chance to form lasting relationships.

Longer [tenure of] a minister...with a parish...[which] better enables parishioners...to know him and what to expect from him.

Chance to try out new styles.

Chance for minister to experiment with new forms of worship in a comfortable setting.

[Chance to] try out and test variety of programs, methodologies, etc.

4. A long pastorate opens up possibilities of greater personal and spiritual growth for both pastor and congregation.

[Chance that] the parson may grow with the parish.

Minister...available over a long period of time...[who] can afford to be patient with your spiritual growth. Really caring and helping you grow in God's love isn't a short term job.

The congregation...able to witness their pastor's growth and benefit from it.

Chance to learn (and change) from errors made.

[Knowledge] that your confidence is fully justi-fied where there are areas of your life which are difficult to share, but sometimes must be shared in order to grow in one's understanding.

Chance to develop "staying power"--commitment through thick and thin.

Chance for an honesty between clergy and laity...to develop.

5. A long pastorate can make possible greater, deeper knowledge of and participation by the pastor in the community outside the parish (local community, professional and ecumenical community, larger denominational community or judicatory) and vice versa.

Good knowledge of the community, its dynamics and resources.

[Ability to] make more effective use of community resources and agencies in counseling and pastoral ministry.

[Chance to become] well known by the community--someone they know to call on.

Enhanced influence in the judicatory structure.

Greater chance [for clergy] to get involved effectively in the outer community (including the ecumenical community).

Knowledge of the city's future or lack of it.

Knowledge of the political atmosphere and realities.

More interest in public and community affairs.

Enhanced ministry to local needs (i.e. nursing homes, prison, etc.).

[Chance for] the church and the town...[to become] his and his family's home also.

6. A long pastorate may have special benefits for both the pastor and his/her family.

Family [which] is settled and children [who] don't have to be uprooted from school by a move.

[Opportunity for] the pastor and his family...[to] put down roots.

Peace of mind for the pastor...security.

[Chance] to be happy in one place over a long period of time.

[Opportunity for] pastor's family [to] grow up in a community.

Benefit to pastor's education and growth.

Pastors added that a long tenure makes it easier to buy and own their own home.

It is clear that the above categories overlap. However, the separate categories each point to a dimension of long pastorates that seems important to highlight. Most could be included under the heading of deepening community.

Potential Disadvantages of a Long Pastorate

Turning to the disadvantages of long pastorates, once again, these need to be seen as potential disadvantages, whose influences may be minimized or aggravated by the quality of the particular ministry (of both pastor and parishioners).

1. A long tenure under a single pastor limits the congregation's exposure to and experience of ministry.

Teaching through sermons...limited or viewpoint too narrow.

Repetition of ideas in sermons.

Narrowness of vision--no new perspectives.

Neglect of certain areas of ministry which he/she is just not good at.

Not as broad a spread of clergy abilities and visions.

[Deterioration in] areas of work in which the pastor is weak.

No opportunity or incentive [for] people who drop out to return.

Parish feel[ing] the need of new leadership.

Pastor's feel[ing of having] nothing more to give.

Problem of personality balance [in] a one pastor church.

2. A long tenure may lead to overidentification between a pastor and parishioners, and of the parish with the pastor. This in turn may make the pastor's eventual departure excessively traumatic for all.

Getting too friendly with parishioners--unable to go against friendship.

[Pastor's attempt] to please parishioners he cares about instead of "rocking the boat."

[Loss of] perspective because [pastor is] too close and too familiar with the people.

[Danger that] when you get to know people too well, they sometimes "turn on you."

More danger of church being seen as synonymous with the clergy.

Time of pastor's leaving...be[ing]...more traumatic and difficult.

3. In a long pastorate, a gap may develop between the pastor and a growing number of parishioners.

Develop[ment of pastor's]...own "entourage" of close parishioners to the exclusion of others.

Probability of divisions within the parish focusing on pastor.

Loss of touch with mainstream parish initiatives or even new ones.

Tendency to concentrate to a growing degree on "special interests," which may not be broadly shared.

Pastor grow[ing] too old to communicate with youth.

Parish...becom[ing] too dependent upon pastor

Tendency on the part of the pastor to do everything himself because it is easier, because he does it better...[which) is dangerous. To say there are no volunteers is true--to do everything yourself makes volunteering unnecessary.

Pastor...tak[ing] over leadership too strongly.

Danger of pastor...[becoming] autonomous.

4. In a long pastorate, there is the danger that a stagnant, ineffective climate can set in. This climate was variously characterized as "getting in a rut," "going stale," "becoming complacent," and "losing flexibility."

Becom[ing] stale in parish projects.

Becom[ing] bored or boring.

[Following] "that's the way we always did it."

Becom[ing] set in ways.

[Having] decreased receptivity to change, loss of flexibility.

Not remain[ing] up-to-date with current theological trends and programs.

Not try[ing] to develop and plan ahead.

Clergy [having] less challenge--less opportunity to grow.

Dealing with the same people, same places and same problems loses its challenge.

Fresh ideas...[becoming] hard to come by.

Spiritual vitality...becom[ing] dormant.

Becoming too comfortable to look for new areas of growth.

[Lack of] aware[ness] of new challenges.

Parishioners...feel[ing]...lack of stimulation.

Losing sight of priorities and/or initial goals.

Stand[ing] in danger of thinking, "We have figured each other out."

Pastor tend[ency] to take the people and the job for granted.

Becom[ing] overly involved in outside activities, which leads to a slowdown in parish duties. Not [having] enough time to do both effectively-- parish suffers.

5. In a long pastorate, there is a greater danger of experiencing burnout.

Discourage[ment] if goals are not materializing.

Stress and burnout with all its obvious and underlying causes.

Total [dedication, making] a certain amount of burnout unavoidable.

Deal[ing] so constantly with life's problems...some spiritual resiliency has to be lost.

Becoming discouraged with self.

Running out of steam.

Los[ing] enthusiasm.

6. As negative influences mount and begin to
outweigh positive influences, a downward spiral may
develop.

Pastor unhapp[iness] leads to development of a
poor rapport...with the congregation.

Families' or individuals'...unhapp[iness] with the
pastor [leads them to]... turn away from the
church.

Troubled relationships [which] may become more
difficult to bear.

Danger of not allowing each other to change, grow,
fail when we least expect it, or succeed in areas
where we had thought no competence pertained.

Loss of gifts from lack of use.

Negative attitudes [which] can be catching.

Alienation of some individuals to the point of no
return.

7. Where things are not going well, a long pastorate can ultimately lead both pastor and parish to
feel that they are helplessly stuck with each other.

Being unhappy where you are, but afraid to make a
change.

Pastor [feeling]...torn between leaving the parish
and injuring his congregation.

Both pastor and parish...feel[ing] locked into the relationship.

Security of position blocking job change or hunt.

Parish...[becoming] saddled with a mediocre pastor too long.

Chance pastor may be tempted never to leave (until forced by retirement).

8. A long pastorate may have some special reduction in benefits for the pastor and the pastor's family.

[Possibility] pastor's financial situation may not improve in same parish.

Diminished possibility for job advancement if pastor stays too long.

A parish...too small for the potential of a minister...so that he does not live up to his potential and take a more important role in the life of the church.

These categories of potential disadvantages overlap and intertwine. Numbers 4 through 7 constitute a sequence contributing to a downward spiral.

Additional Reflections

Virtually all the disadvantages of a LTP can be surmounted, yet few of the advantages are available to clergy who remain in a congregation for only a short period of time;

Clergy in an effective LTP have developed the capacity to deal productively with conflict;

The Clergy Burnout Inventory revealed a higher degree of burnout than expected (one out of four

clergy in the study were bordering on burnout, one
out of six was in burnout, one out of ten was in
the extreme phase) and burnout was identified by
laity as the greatest disadvantage of LTP;

Negative assumptions about LTP have helped create
a negative self-image for the clergy in them;

Participant movement did not have to mean geo-
graphical relocation; participants may have just
as validly gained additional perspective on their
present LTP and assistance in planning next steps
toward a more creative and productive ministry;

Congregations which foster healthy LTPs care for
their own members as well as others outside the
congregation, accept the clergy as human, allow
room for failure, have a willingness to work with
the clergy on common goals, use problem solving
rather than blame in dealing with troublesome
issues and are open to new input, ideas and
members;

When both clergy and laity understand the phenomena of gap development, they can be creative in
working against its unhealthy effects.

Generally, spouses in this study, all women,
were found to be emotionally healthy women who have
made peace in a positive way with their role as
clergy wives; they were open, trusting, and willing
to share their experiences. Spouses were clear about
the advantages of a LTP for themselves, including the
building of support system and the establishment of
tradition. Spouses had less feelings of LTP guilt
and sense of clergy failure than did their clergy
husbands. In most cases, their future was intimately
integrated with that of their husband and, whatever
their vocational situation or aspiration, they acknowledged that their husband's call to a new church
took precedence over their own career plans.

III. Basic Theories Developed

A gap develops between growing number of
parishioners and the clergy----➤a stagnant ineffective climate sets in----➤
clergy (and also dedicated parish leaders) experience burnout----➤a downward
spiral is experienced as negative influences outweigh positive influences----➤
over time, pastor and parish begin to
feel stuck with each other.

Many, if not all, the pastors had experienced this
downward sequence in some measure, and had used a
variety of influences and resources to reverse the
downward spiral. The pastorate--especially the long
pastorate--can be viewed as a continual battle
between opposing forces: those which alienate, which
stifle growth and health, and which are ultimately
destructive of a productive ministry, and those which
make for healing and renewal. These forces are complex, involve the total parish system, and, although
the pastor carries significant shaping responsibility, cannot be simply laid at the door of the pastor. In short-term ministries, the pastor may move
before a serious downward spiral takes hold. Neither
pastor nor congregation in such short pastorates have
an opportunity to learn what's needed to bring healing and renewal into a stagnant or toxic situation.
However, for a long pastorate to remain healthy or
to recover from declining periods, it is crucial for
both pastor and congregation to know what makes for
health and renewal. Viewed from this perspective, a
healthy long-tenured pastorate may be seen as the
outcome of a joint pastor/parishioner spiritual

pilgrimage, which calls upon all parties for "eternal vigilance" and for profound mutual caring and commitment to those qualities which make for such a healthy ministry.

The Gap

Trust Development

As we learned about the dynamics of long-tenured pastorates, some unique facts emerged. One of the most significant theoretical insights had to do with congregational effectiveness in a pastorate longer than ten years. Contrary to what might be assumed, unless in the first ten years of a pastorate certain things happen, either accidentally or intentionally, the general productiveness of a congregation begins to diminish. This happens even though personal trust and affection between individual parishioners and the pastor increases dramatically.

On a graph, a line representing interpersonal trust between pastor and individual parishioners will grow higher and higher. But, a second line, representing the effectiveness of the congregation's life, or corporate trust, trust of the people in their pastor's ability to help them be a dynamic, growing parish, will curve downward. A growing gap between the lines occurs.

We are referring to healthy long pasorates in which both clergy and laity feel good about each other. No gap occurs unless there are some powerfully strong and positive interactions in the dynamic between pastor and people.

Through heightened trust, a piece of this relationship keeps on getting better and better

while another piece begins to decline through unfulfilled expectations

44

Individual versus Corporate Trust

As parishioners' personal trust of their pastor
continues to rise the longer he/she is in that
office, their trust of him/her as the corporate
executive (who will solve the parish's problems and
make it thrive) begins to decline. Through a strong
pastoral ministry, clergy often continue to endear
themselves to members of the congregation as they
minister to parishioners through the trials,
tribulations, and joys of life. At the same time,
parishioners' trust in the pastor's ability to lead
the congregation out of its accumulated difficulties
onto new levels of achievement begins to diminish.

In the beginning of most pastorates, parishioners
usually expect great things to happen in the parish
through the new pastor. They anticipate the emerg-
ence of new growth and energy in parish life; their
corporate trust in the new pastor is high. At the
same time, they may be unsure of this new pastor's
ability to handle the deeper issues of their personal
lives; their individual trust in him or her may be
low. Their individual trust grows as they perceive
the new pastor ministering to them through individual
and family crisis periods. (See John Fletcher's
Religious Authenticity in the Clergy [Alban Institute, 1975] for a helpful theory that sheds light on
this stage in pastor-parish relationships.)

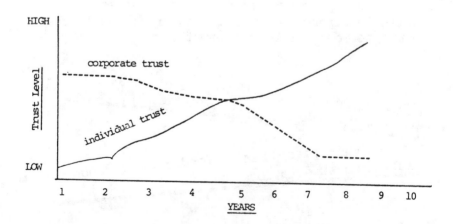

At some point the lines converge and cross with
individual trust continuing to grow through effective
pastoral care, and corporate trust diminishing as
parishioners' conscious or unconscious expectations
for parish growth and vitality begin to be frustrated.

Why does this take place? When the pastor has
shared at least one major crisis with each parishioner and/or family, then the people of the parish
will tend, out of their personal trust in the pastor,
to delegate congregational power to him/her. Signs
of this might be infrequent new program starts,
lessened vitality and growth, inability to deal with
conflict constructively, diminishing of new lay leadership, burnout of reliable lay leadership. Yet, all
the time this is happening, the pastor and people
will feel more and more tied to one another in personal ways, more like a family, more mutually
trusting and caring.

We tested this idea with the sixteen pastors and
spouses who took part in the New England seminars.
Their initial reaction was rather chilly, an under-
standable response since the theory appears to assume
that all long pastorates go stale. After considering
the idea for several months, they came back with
somewhat different reactions. During the second
stage of the program, we asked them to respond to
what we have come to call "The Gap Theory." Some of
these responses follow:

Individual trust is good, but the church as a
whole starts drawing back, withholding support,
blaming me for all the problems.

The longer the pastorate, the more one operates on
the basis of assumption, habit and pattern.

The mandate that brought you there no longer
exists. A new mandate needs to emerge and be
dealt with. Gap: old mandate--new mandate.

The quality and type of feedback had potential for
keeping the gap closed.

As years go by the feedback needs to get at the more subtle issues that drain energy away from parishioners.

The gap exists between liking people have for a pastor, yet the fear of trusting him with feedback or being too frightened to—especially since he's been there a long time.

There is parish commitment to a leader (lots of trust) rather than commitment to their own community with priest as leader.

As intimacy develops, organization can suffer.

There is a gap between individual trust and relationship versus congregational trust

All of these comments reflect a thoughtful validation of the real danger of the "Gap," and the need for its impact to be recognized and dealt with. In those long pastorates into which it is most difficult to breathe life, what has happened is that interpersonal intimacy has grown until the people and pastor are truly like a family, with all the positive/negative possibilities this implies. Yet congregational effectiveness has diminished. And many feel helpless to do anything about it! As one Diocesan staff member, not involved in this project, said: "There are some long, long pastorates that my boss (the Bishop) won't touch with a ten foot pole with any kind of intervention. And among those are some of our most difficult situations."

Had the "Gap" not had a chance to develop in those parishes, the story might well have been quite different. Is this "Gap" a predictable event in all long pastorates? Does the deepening affection pastor and people have for each other usually impede their corporate growth and development in the long run?

It is the conclusion of our research team that the "Gap" between corporate trust and individual trust will tend to widen in all long pastorates, effective

or ineffective, unless both pastor and parish cons-
ciously and vigilantly work against it. The evidence
from our study supports this conclusion:

The more a pastor is loved and supported by parishioners, the more painfully aware he/she will be
of the fact that changes in the parish will hurt
certain people. Clergy admit this fact tends to
make them think twice before facing the tough decisions that growth demands.

Parishioners admit that it is far more difficult
for them to share negative feelings with their
pastor when they have come to value highly the
loving individual ministry she/he gives to them.
"We love dear old Rev. Smith. He's the one that
helped us face through the pain of Dad's death. I
couldn't bring myself to tell him his sermons are
getting a little old and boring."

The more loved and trusted a pastor becomes on an
interpersonal level, the more parishioners defer
to him/her on corporate issues. People who feel
less need for pastoral support maintain a more
appropriate balance between pastor power and people power in decision making areas.

Clergy often come to a parish because of the
challenge to get things moving and certain things
accomplished. Once these changes are in place,
however, there is an inclination to settle into
deepening pastoral care of parishioners on an
individual and family basis.

Gap Prevention Dynamics

The "Gap Theory" is not a final pronouncement about
the fate of all pastorates of ten years and longer.
While certain dynamics of familiarity and trust will
make congregational health seem more and more difficult to maintain in all long pastorates, we have
discovered that there are some elements that can

exist in a pastor/parish relationship that will narrow and even close the "Gap" we have described.

We found exceptions to the "Gap." These exceptions do not occur because pastors and parishioners were warned of the likelihood of the "Gap" and did something to keep it from happening. The exceptions exist in parishes where early healthy relationships and dynamics have laid the foundation for strong interpersonal trust (between the pastor and individual parishioners) and strong corporate trust (between "the people" and the pastor). The former can and often does exist without the latter; the latter cannot exist without the former. In these long pastorates where both kinds of trust exist, it appears that one or more of three processes has taken place within the first ten years of that pastorate.

1. Effective Crisis Management. The pastor and people have learned, often through hard experience, how to manage crises well. Most of the pastors who took part in the New England study began their pastorates just at the beginning or in the middle of the civil rights/peace crises of the 1960s. It is no accident that, over ten years later, they are all in the same pastorates. The stories that unfolded revealed many people who managed well during those difficult times, for all those congregations were affected by these crises, and they have held on to the health that came from learning their crisis strategies well.

2. Shared Vision. The pastor and people together have made significant changes in the way they make decisions, manage their ongoing life, and see their vision of their future. In one of the most vital long pastorates we observed, the vestry is chosen by lottery each year. This has been done since the beginning of this rectorate. The decision is reaffirmed regularly; it is reowned in common by the rector and the people; it is celebrated as unique. It is one of the primary reasons why their relationship remains vital after sixteen years. Other healthy long pastorates revealed early decisions to incorporate new people into the leadership

life of the congregation, a reshaping of their decision making structures, or a joint struggle to gain
a new vision of what they should be as a people of
faith. When such organic processes are shared by
pastor and people, reaffirmed and reowned regularly,
and cherished as "their own," a lasting vibrancy in
their corporate life is generated. This process also
must include a willingness of pastor and people to
test their nature and being as a congregation. This
willingness to risk looking at themselves, no matter
how long they have been together, demonstrates their
health as a congregation.

    3. <u>Life Renewal</u>. The pastor and the people have
undergone some kind(s) of spiritual and/or pro-
grammatic renewal together. Some long pastorates
have vitality because a new sense of faith has
claimed the shared life of that congregation.
This might be a new vision about how their resources are to be channeled. It might be a new
urgency about evangelism, social action, education, liturgy, etc. It includes regular ways in
which the congregation is "recharged" to do its
mission.

    No two congregations are alike. No two pastorates
are alike. But we can generalize that in those congregations where a healthy combination of interpersonal trust with the pastor and corporate trust with
him/her exists, one or more of these three kinds of
processes have also existed.

The Downward Spiral

One of the realities of long pastorates is that a
certain percentage of clergy are caught in a downward spiral. They are burned out; they have little
going for them. Their congregations are not happy
with their ministry. Parishioners give off signals
that they would like them to move. These clergy have
tried to move, but have been incapable of attracting
a call elsewhere. Each rejection from another parish
sends them even deeper into dismay and depression.
Because its too painful to be turned down time after
time, they stop trying.

Discontent with their ministry further erodes their
confidence, so they continue to perform poorly. In
such cases, there are often dysfunctional aspects in
home life as well; there isn't a solid support base
even on the home front. Many such clergy become
desperate, irrational and/or unresponsive. Everything suggests they are not suited to the ministry.
They appear incapable of self-improvement.

It's long pastorates like these that drive church
executives crazy. While their pastoral side calls
for softness, leniency and caring, their corporate
executive side demands these clergy be moved out of
office and replaced by more capable clergy. Many
executives are not skilled in dealing with this
complex and contradictory situation, and communicate
to these clergy that they are "a problem" to the
judicatory and driving them even deeper into despair.

Pastorates like these give long pastorates a bad
reputation. No matter how positive we can be about
long pastorates, every executive, every pastor and
lay person knows of a case like those described above
that shade the positive glow of good long pastorates. For the most part, clergy in such failing
situations hope for rescue by their executive or
another parish. In most cases this just doesn't
happen. The only solution is for them to dig themselves out of the hole in which they find themselves. To get a call elsewhere, they will first
need to have something positive going for them in
their current parish. We have the personal testimony
of one clergyman in a long pastorate who did just
that--reversed the downward spiral and got enough
going for himself that he could move. His rock
bottom was his acknowledgement that he was a con-
firmed alcoholic. His stepping stone up was his
ability to reach out for help. Therapy helped him
lick his alcoholism and slowly, but surely, he
tackled his other problems one at a time. At the end
of this process he was offered a job as an agency
alcohol counselor.

Long-tenured clergy caught in a downward spiral,
with burnout a primary factor, clearly need help,

help which is something other than covering for them,
than protecting them from the truth about their
lives, help which gives them the support and direction they need to face their demons and fight them
one by one. Clergy who can't reach out for help
normally don't make it. They end up either being
fired or given early retirement by their parishioners, or experiencing several years of hostility or
bare tolerance from their congregation.

We have yet to learn of any model that middle
judicatories have developed to intervene early enough
in these situations in a firm, forthright way. It
is politically hazardous for a judicatory executive
to intervene in a parish situation where there has
been no request for help from either clergy or
laity. Not to intervene, however, means waiting and
watching the situation disintegrate to the point
where people have no choice but to ask for help. By
then, the situation may have deteriorated so badly
that any kind of therapeutic help and efforts for
reconciliation will no longer work. If such a downward spiral is to be reversed before it reaches this
point, the intervention strategy may need to be a
radical one, involving great energy and many resources. Such intervention requires:

Therapy and other training opportunities;

A special kind of consultation with the parish;

A new type and quality of support, not only for
the clergy, but also for their families.

In darker moments, many clergy in long pastorates
fear the downward spiral will happen to them. The
one clear preventative is engaging in good self-care
habits which prevent burnout in the first place. In
preparation for parish ministry, we have not been
taught good self-care habits nor have we been given
support and encouragement to take care of ourselves
on a regular basis. Self-care involves our use of
deliberate strategies to maintain physical, emotional

and spiritual health. More specifically, it calls
for:

Time for spiritual formation;
Good nutrition;
Exercise;
More relaxation;
Development of more support for oneself;
Time to enrich family life;
Personal interests unrelated to work;
Assertiveness training;
Effective time management;
Therapy when indicated;
Sabbatical leave;
Methods for spiritual development;
More laughter.

To prepare for times of crisis we need to have
developed the ability to work our way out of a hole.
Through it all, we need to value ourselves highly
enough so that we refuse to allow burnout to devas-
tate our lives.

Survival in a long pastorate with our physical,
emotional and spiritual health intact implies:
working hard at it and carefully monitoring the
work/leisure balance;

Engaging in good self-care habits;

Having much Grace available in one's ministry.

Long-Tenured Pastorate Personality Type

By far the majority of clergy attracted to a long
pastorate are feeling oriented people, according to
the Myers-Briggs Type Indicator (M.B.T.I.) (See
Instruments Section in Appendix.) It is our experience that feeling oriented people are more vulnerable
to the development of a "Gap" in a long pastorate than
thinking oriented people. We used the M.B.T.I. with
thirty-three clergy involved in this Alban Institute

research project and with an additional thirty-nine involved in two other long-term pastorate studies.

Our attention was immediately drawn to the high proportion of feeling oriented clergy involved in our studies. Out of a total of seventy-two clergy in a pastorate of ten years or more, sixty-five (or 90.5%) emerged on the feeling side of the M.B.T.I.

The center for Application of Psychological Type, Inc. in Gainesville, Florida possesses research data that indicates that in the profession of clergy, F's (feeling oriented persons) outnumber T's (thinking oriented persons) by as many as three to one. Since religion is concerned with values, it is reasonable to expect that religious life would appeal to those people whose judgments are most influenced by values. Even this high proportion of "F" clergy, however, is not nearly as high as the number of F's in our long-term pastorate study. This makes sense when one gives it some thought:

Feeling types tend to become very attached to people and communities;

Feeling types have a more difficult time saying "goodbye;"

At times the skill of a feeling oriented person serves a parish well over the long haul;

Feeling types are much more in touch with people when they are hurt and upset, are motivated to try to do something about the hurt or upset and usually have the skills to heal these pains.

On the liability side, feeling type clergy tend to enjoy working with people rather than with administrative detail. They have a greater tendency to slide into effective pastoral ministries, allowing organizational issues related to health and growth to go by the board. Feeling oriented clergy, following their natural inclinations, spend more time and energy on interpersonal relations than they do on corporate issues or on cold and impersonal organizational concerns. When a parish focuses on strong directional goals, some people will naturally be disturbed. The feeling oriented pastor will feel their pain much more acutely than a thinking oriented pastor. We can see why there would be a slightly greater inclination for feeling clergy to spend more time on individual pastoral concerns vis-a-vis tough organizational issues. According to the "Gap" theory, this very strength becomes a potential downfall in their ministry.

Thinking type clergy tend to be more goal and competence oriented and to press organizational concerns, yet to be less aware of the feelings of people in the change effort. Being more competence oriented, and having less difficulty with farewells, once certain objectives have been fulfilled they tend to move on to new challenges in other parishes. We surmise that they would be less capable of surviving a long pastorate because they have fewer skills and capabilities in identifying and dealing with discontent or hurt feelings in the parish. Should they have skills to compensate for this deficiency, they would be well suited for an effective long pastorate with their ability to keep growth and organizational issues moving.

We wonder whether the church can expect all its clergy to be equally skilled in both of these important aspects of parish life. Will not each pastor have greater skill, interest, propensity for one vis-a-vis the other? Are those who can manage well both personal/pastoral concerns and corporate/organizational concerns more the exception than the rule? If so, what are the ways parishes and judicatories can compensate for a lack of balance in any pastorate between these two dimensions of parish life?

In addition to the "F" function in these clergy, we also noted a higher than normal proportion of judging types than perceptive types. Of the clergy tested 71.9% favored judging over perceiving, an indication that these clergy value structure and

order more than they do spontaneity and openness.
Once again this strength they bring to their ministries in terms of stability and continuity can
become their liability in their undervaluing change
and renewal.

In summary, the "Gap" between individual trust and
corporate trust is likely to widen in all long pastorates, but especially in parishes where clergy are
first and foremost lovers, who learn to care deeply
for their people. The most potent strength they
bring to parish ministry can become their nemesis
over the long haul. The same holds true for clergy
in long pastorates who tend to value structure and
order over spontaneity and change.

It is our strong recommendation that the clergy
and congregations involved in a long pastorate remain
vigilant as to the potential "Gap" that invariably
will threaten an effective pastor/parish dynamic.

In the Alban Institute Interim Pastorate Project,
we also built a profile of clergy best suited for Interim ministries (six to eighteen months preparation of congregations for more permanent ministers).
These clergy were desirous of adventure, very goal
oriented, comfortable with conflict, bored with
long-term ministries and living in a style congruent
with such short-term ministry.

An appropriate analogy can be made to the "Hillside People," who build their homes high on the
mountain so they can overlook great vistas. These
are the seed planters who get bored easily and seek
new challenges. Their eye is on the broad picture.
Adventure and newness are important to them.

If interim clergy are "Hillside People," then
clergy in long pastorates might be termed "Pondside
People," who build their homes over a pond where
hills slope gently down to focus attention on a
small, specific piece of real estate. These folks
are continually fascinated by life right under their
noses, intrigued with new forms of life revealed in
day to day living, caught up in the drama of the life
of the pond, constantly plumbing the depth in the
meaning of the life around them.

Harold Dean, a Unitarian minister in a fifteen-year long pastorate, says:

> The longer I stay in this place, the more I see. I continue to be fascinated with the revelation of new life going on right in our midst, and the steady unfolding of people I work with. New possibilities seem to open up for me on a regular basis in my current scene.

In the future we hope to develop a survey instrument to measure clergy's propensity to be either "Hillside" or "Pondside" pastors. This might help clergy plan their careers in a more informed way and assist them to come to terms with phenomena which occur in frequent moves or in long pastorates.

Support Pillars of Healthy Long Pastorates

From our four-year study of long pastorates our team has arrived at a concept of five support pillars of a healthy, dynamic long pastorate. This concept assumes that the pastor is adequately managing the normal pastoral activities of preaching, crisis ministry, administration, etc. These five pillars are:

A Healthy, Dynamic Long Pastorate

| Monitoring the "Gap" between individual trust and corporate trust | Keeping oneself an alive and growing person, especially spiritually | Maintaining and soliciting quality feedback from the parish | Watching for burnout-- good self-care habits and practices | Seeing that the democratic representative process is maintained in the parish |

Three of the above five fit into the "Gap"
Theory. In addition to the "Gap" between individual
and corporate trust, a second "Gap" can develop
between the amount and quality of feedback one needs
for effective ministry and the amount and quality of
feedback that one allows, will hear, or is available. A third "Gap" can occur when only a handful of
people have input into key parish decisions vis-a-vis
having all people's interests represented--a difference between all factions and/or interest groups and
only special people and interests being represented
in the parish decision making process. The remaining
two pillars deal with personal and professional self
care. Keeping oneself on a growing edge intellectu-
ally, emotionally and spiritually is one part; monitoring one's stress and engaging in good self-care
habits is the second.

Monitoring the Gap

The most important potential "Gap" between pastor and
people is the "Gap" between individual trust and
corporate trust. It is the most deceptive and the
hardest with which to deal.

Since the development of our original hypothesis
about the "Gap," we have continued to test it and to
seek its further implications. We asked participants
in our long pastorate study symposia about the other
"Gaps" in long pastorates. Here are some that
emerged:

The "Gap" between available feedback and feedback of
the quality and type needed to do the job.

As years go by...feedback [is needed]...to uncover
the more subtle forces that drain energy away from
parishioners.

There is a communications barrier that seems to
develop over time between (a) pastor and people,
and (b) pastor and staff.

The "Gap" between the pastor's "in group" (lay leaders that cluster around the pastor) and the rest of the congregation.

> Parishioners...fade out of the picture after the pastor has crossed them off as laity who offered little leadership.

> Pastors...[are] more concerned with developing new relationships than with healing old relationships.

The "Gap" between the pastor's continuing to be challenged to offer his or her best to the congregation and his becoming more discouraged, more routinized, less patient, less committed, less enthusiastic.

> The longer the pastorate, the more one begins to operate on the basis of assumption, habit and pattern.

> As clergy's level of excitement about the work decreases, they become less patient with the day to day pinches and crunches.

The "Gap" between old priorities that have been fulfilled and new ones that are as yet unmet.

> The mandate that brought me here no longer exists. A new mandate needs to be stated for the pastor.

These are but a few of the alternative ways clergy and laity have viewed the gap that developed in their long pastorate. Remaining open to the unique ways in which a gap can develop between pastor and people is also a way of responding effectively to this phenomenon. It's very important to remember that our theory of the gap developing between Individual trust and Corporate trust in most long pastorates is just that —a theory. Your data may suggest a different theory.

We recommend inviting a group of trusted lay people to assist in the struggle to keep the "Gap" closed. In our workshops we discovered that when both clergy and laity understand the phenomenon of "Gap" development, both can be quite creative in working against its devastating effects. One possible approach is the formation of a pastor/parish relations committee, which would focus its energy on the pastor/parish dynamic. This group could include among its tasks a yearly assessment of potential gaps and could then work collaboratively to overcome them.

Under certain circumstances we would recommend the use of an outside facilitator, possibly a judicatory executive or staff member, to evaluate the congregation's sense of the "Gap."

The pastor, however, needs to be most vigilant about the "Gap." Because of the possible self-deception in such an evaluation we recommend some support from outside the family or parish to help in this monitoring. Explaining the "Gap" theory to trusted colleagues or a peer support group would help in "holding one's feet to the fire" on the problem.

Sustaining One's Personal, Professional, Spiritual Growing Edge

When we asked for advantages and disadvantages of a long pastorate on our laity questionnaire, out of 144 responses, seventy-one or forty-nine percent of the replies centered around:

Going stale;
Becoming complacent;
Going to seed;
Not growing with the congregation;
Becom[ing] set in ways;
[Losing] flexibility;
Not keeping abreast of the times.

Almost fifty percent of the responses dealt with either the fear or the experience of having their pastor "go stale." We shared this data with clergy

in our North Carolina seminar. It was from their
laity that we had acquired this statistic. Most did
not feel they had gone stale or become complacent.

Were these lay people expressing a fear of what
might happen to their clergy, or were these expres-
sions grounded in reality?

Maintaining one's growing edge is no easy task in
a long pastorate. There are all the signs that
things are going well and that one need not worry.
Besides, there seem to be many more important things
to worry about than going to continuing education
conferences, reading or engaging in doctoral studies.

Statistically only twenty percent of Protestant
clergy in this country engage in a minimal one week
of continuing education seminars each year. It is
our hope that the remaining eighty percent are not in
long pastorates. One can appear to get away with an
avoidance of personal/professional development if one
moves about every few years. One can make it on re-
runs of sermons, Bible studies, etc., and on general
knowledge of parish life. It's a different story in
a long pastorate. People, coming back year after
year, want to be renewed and refreshed. This is only
possible when a pastor is also renewing and refresh-
ing him/herself.

Continual spiritual development of pastors is of
special concern. Levinson's The Seasons of a Man's
Life[3] states that persons often outgrow their
mentors in six to eight years. The pupil who has
learned all he can from his mentor must move on to
find other mentors. How is it possible for a pastor
to be a spiritual mentor for growing people over a
ten to twelve year span? The pastor must constantly
grow spiritually him/herself.

Another way to ask the question is: "How can a
congregation continue to grow spiritually over the
years?" The most obvious answer is either to have a
series of spiritually mature clergy or to have one
leader who is always pursuing his/her spiritual
growing edge.

It is easy to get swallowed up by the day to day

activities of a parish, ignoring these special
needs. Yet, leadership means envisioning the future,
showing the way by personal example and practices and
allowing others to catch the vision and excitement.

Staying alive and healthy spiritually will not
likely take place unless clergy have disciplines
which keep them tuned into their spiritual journey.
For most of us, seminary education did little to
prepare us to stay alive spiritually. Any disciplines, practices, rituals, "rule of life" that we
adopted we had to pick up on our own. The three most
common spiritual disciplines (prayer, scriptual reflection and worship) are less likely to be personally helpful to clergy because they are the tools of
pastoral ministry. Many clergy feel that they pray
so much for others, they don't need a prayer life of
their own. Scripture reading is usually related to
sermon and lesson preparation. Since as clergy we
become experts at conducting worship, we are usually
less able ourselves to worship. To keep spiritual
life rich and meaningful, most clergy need spiritual
disciplines over and above these three, disciplines
that engage them on a daily, weekly, yearly and
"sabbatical year" basis. Without these, they are
guided by their subjective nature of their feelings
regarding religious practice. When it doesn't feel
right they don't do it.

Spiritual disciplines that have been found helpful
to others are:

Meditation, involving some instruction on type,
use and practice;

Journal Keeping, also involving some special instruction;

Fasting on juice for one to five days;

Tracking One's Dreams, which before Aristotle and
Aquinas were the common way God spoke to his people;

Retreats/Days of Silence, especially helpful in
settings such as monasteries or retreat centers;

Yoga, Tai Chi, Running for these people who are
more easily able to become centered when body
movement is involved;

Spiritual Friend/Mentor Contract with a respected colleague for support and consultation on spiritual growth.

We highly recommend that clergy in a long pastorate isolate one or two spiritual disciplines suited to their personality and life style, receive some special training in those disciplines, and then gain whatever support they need to pursue those practices on a regular basis.

All of this takes time and can occur with greater regularity with parish support. When moving into a new pastorate, it is very important to build a support base for one's personal/professional/ spiritual growth and development. Without this, both clergy and congregation are losers. The incongruous situation of laity fearing that their pastor is going stale and yet refusing to give time off, and/or financial support for personal growth and development, must be confronted. Laity need to provide support for the pastor's regular time off for the exercise of spiritual disciplines.

Our final concern is for sabbatical leave for clergy in long pastorates. It is ludicrous to believe that year after year a pastor can be continually helpful and occasionally profound in weekly Sunday sermons without periodic opportunities to get away for an extended time.

This study has pointed us more and more toward the need (in addition to vacations) for parish clergy to engage in a three month sabbatical every few years. Though sabbaticals are not without their own built-in difficulties, time spent on travel, rest, new experiences, disciplined study, etc. can add a special zest and sparkle to the ministry of a long-tenured pastor. Both congregation and pastor should plan these well in advance. When clergy believe that the congregation has as much to gain from a sabbatical as they themselves do, they will be more likely to press for it. To help in this pursuit, we recommend Learning to Share the Ministry,[4] by James R. Adams and Celia A. Hahn.

Maintaining and Soliciting Quality Feedback

We have found in our study that lack of feedback is a
danger in a long pastorate. Yet, the longer pastor
and parishioners stay together, the more difficult it
is for them to give and receive feedback. This is
especially true if there is growing affection between
the two. It is a simple fact of life that it is most
difficult to give painful feedback to a close friend
or family member.

This was substantiated by comments shared by key
people in this study, many of which pointed to a lack
of candid communication between pastor and people.

> The pastor knows the people so well, is too close
> to them, in a sense, 'owns them,' so that all
> perspective is lost.

> The clergy take over the leadership and are
> allowed to do anything with little questioning
> from the governing board or laity.

> Long term personal attachments influence decision
> making; one can't go against friendships.

Clergy in the study also noted that feedback
became more difficult the longer one stayed.

> As years go by, the feedback needs to get at the
> more subtle issues that drain energy away from the
> parishioners.

> [There is] the liking people have for a pastor,
> yet their fear of trusting him/her with feedback
> ...especially since he/she's been there a long
> time.

> [I am aware] of sensing the trust level erode as
> well as finding it harder to get honest feedback.

Clarity over the value and necessity of solid
feedback in a long pastorate prompted us to solicit

lay views of the barriers to clergy receiving clear
and candid feedback on their ministry over extended
periods. The 132 responses to that question fell into
the following categories:

40 - Parishioner problems in expressing concerns
directly to their pastor (a whole range of
communication problems);

32 - Pastors not open to feedback--lack of
openness to newness or change;

18 - Fear of offending pastors because of close
personal relationships;

17 - Miscellaneous/unclear responses;

10 - Perception by clergy or congregation of
pastors' exalted position;

10 - Existence of special groups within the
congregation;

5 - No barriers.

Fifty-one percent of these laity said barriers to
candid feedback to clergy lie with lay people while
twenty-four percent said barriers were the fault of
clergy. Only four percent said there were no barriers to clergy receiving clear and candid feedback
from laity over extended periods.

What difficulties related to candid feedback are
intrinsic to the interaction between a religious
authority and parish member over time? Are there
barriers that are not found in other relationships?
Whatever the difficulties, they appear to become
greater the longer pastor and people stay together.

Overcoming barriers to candid feedback in a long
pastorate requires skill and determination. Several
principles should be observed in this effort.

1. Most laity, if given a choice, would rather not

become engaged in giving feedback to their pastor.
It's not what they want or need to do. In their
secular work settings evaluation experiences are
usually negative. In addition, they would rather not
see the clay feet of their pastor. They need him/her
to be strong, loving and available. Involvement with
his/her weaknesses and vulnerabilities may detract
from that.

Given this reluctance by laity, we should not
expect them to offer feedback to the pastor freely or
voluntarily. Lay people need to be assured that the
process of giving feedback to the pastor is well
managed, with solid leadership at the center of the
experience. They need to know that the feedback is
valued, even solicited by the pastor.

2. The use of a skilled outside facilitator can do
much to improve the quality of feedback given to a
pastor. in addition to bringing skill and leadership
to the process, an outside facilitator can act as a
stabilizing force. Since a pastor is seen as the
chief authority figure in the parish, when she/he is
being evaluated, many may become quite anxious about
"who is in charge here?" They may distrust the mo-
tives of certain lay leaders if the pastor gets too
much negative feedback.

The pastor also needs to know that someone with
skill and care is managing the process. Without this
trust she/he may become defensive rather than accepting and trusting of the process.
3. Since being a pastor is more a role than a specific set of functions, it is important that she/he not
be evaluated only on parish functions (preaching,
teaching, administrating, etc.). Evaluation of performance of those functions may not get at the es-
sence of what the congregation needs and wants from
their pastor.

Watching for Burnout

If "rustout," complacency, going to seed, going
stale, etc. is a problem in long pastorates, so is

the opposite extreme, namely clergy overextension to
the point of burnout. The skill required in long
pastorates is that of being able to live between the
extremes of burnout and "rustout."

Burnout

Effective long pastorates
lived between these two
hazards.

Rustout

Some stress to keep one on the creative growing edge
is needed, however.

Burnout is a malady to be avoided at all costs.
It is a devastating disease that dries up a person's
life energy and spirit. It is marked by three separate but related phenomena:

Physical and emotional depletion--
Symptoms: difficulty in getting out of bed in the
in the morning, difficulty maintaining energy for any
parish activity, feeling overpeopled and wanting more
than anything to be left alone;

Cynicism about parishioners, parish and people in
general--Symptoms: feeling people will never change
or grow up, losing confidence in the parish's ability
to grow or change, hanging on to remorse, anger, pain
of past events;

<u>Self-blame for all problems</u>--Symptoms: becoming
cynical about oneself being loaded down with one's
own guilt and/or anger, frequently depreciating
oneself/"turning the sword inward".

Burnout can, over time, reduce someone with
health, vision and vitality to a cynical, bitter,
petty bureaucrat. Clergy affected by burnout end up
dull, hollow, listless men and women. They are able
to function at some level as parish clergy, but all
the spark and vitality has gone out of their
ministry. They've stopped having fun at what they
do. The Gospel is always best proclaimed when it
comes from people who are enjoying themselves and
life.
In this profession, burnout is lethal. It is
nearly impossible to proclaim effectively the good
news of the Gospel when one is burned out. What
emerges is a double message. The words speak of
Grace, but all else bespeaks tragedy, brokenness and
depression. McLuhan is right: "The medium is the
message. If the medium is a burned out clergy person, the message is, "Don't take the Gospel seriously
or you'll end up like me."

Maintaining the Parish Representative/Democratic Process

We have noted that frequently, the longer a pastor is
in place, the more power she/he has. The chance for
this to occur is even greater when the pastor is well
loved and trusted. It simply is easier for parishioners to defer important decisions to the pastor,
trusting that she/he will "do right by them."

In most mainline denominational parishes, there
are essentially two congregtions. Congregation A is
that core group of people who contribute about eighty
percent of the budget and are found in eighty percent
of parish leadership roles, even though they
represent only approximately twenty percent of the parish.

This phenomenon can be diagrammed as follows:

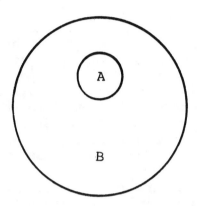

This inner core, congregation A, runs the parish.
Congregation B is there mainly to worship and participate in what the parish offers.

Our experience is that over time Congregation A
reflects the age, values, life style and theology of
the pastor. This mainly occurs in healthy long pastorates where the pastor is respected and well-
liked. It is usually not true in difficult pastorates where the pastor is in trouble with the parish.
In those cases there often is an adversarial relationship between Congregation A and the pastor.

The longer a pastor remains in a parish the more
homogeneous Congregation A becomes. Those who dis-
like the pastor or disagree with his/her style of
ministry normally retreat to the periphery of the
parish to wait for a pastor who is more congruent
with their expectations of a religious leader. In
long pastorates these folks need to wait a long time,
and some will leave the parish unless the congregation takes special pains to regard their input
seriously.

The process of congregation A becoming more homogeneous is a slow, subtle one. The pastor need not
be politically active to ensure that all his/her
friends and cohorts get nominated to leadership
positions. The parish seems to sense who will work
best with the pastor and elects those who are most
"like" him/her. Thus vestries, sessions, boards,
over time reflect the pastor's viewpoints and perspectives. The flip side can also be true. The
election of a congregational slate that definitely
breaks this mold usually marks the beginning of a new
set of parish tensions. This can be a healthy move
on the part of the parish; it usually means that one
faction in the congregation which does not like the
way things are being run has made their move for
change.

Homogeneity of Congregation A can also take place
in another way with either the conscious or
unconscious involvement of the pastor. Whether real-
ized or not, clergy are power brokers in the parish,
empowering some lay people and depowering others by
their choice of whom they invite to become more deeply involved in parish life. Most likely they are
unconscious of this empowering/depowering when they
say either, I like you, why don't you come in closer
and serve on the committee?" or "I don't like you or
your viewpoint. I will not recommend you for a committee appointment." This happens subtly until one
day clergy find they like everyone in parish leadership roles. This may be the beginning of the disen-
franchisement of certain subgroups or viewpoints
within the parish.

Every parish is made up of a large number of cau-
cuses or subgroups. Many of these are compatible
with one another although there are usually some
whose viewpoints diverge considerably from others.
Over time those in unpopular subgroups become more
and more isolated from the decision making mechanisms
in the parish, particularly when they cease to have
an advocate in the pastor.

Decision making is easiest when people of similar
viewpoints and perspectives occupy positions on the

board or committees. The implementation of those decisions may be more difficult as divergent viewpoints get expressed in passive or active resistance from other people. Those who don't agree with decisions either don't participate or refuse financial support to those projects. Usually only those with high verbal skills will directly take on a board or committee when they don't agree with decisions.

An alternative mode of decision making is to ensure that the divergent viewpoints find expression on boards or committees prior to a decision. This usually makes decision making long and painful. However, when the committee or board has done its work well, implementation of these decisions usually flows much more easily. People who feel their perspectives have been heard and respected are much more willing to support decisions.

These are only a few ways in which parishioners can become more and more disenfranchised in a long pastorate. The more comfortable people are with a pastor, the more they will find ways to defer decisions to him/her. Even clergy who try to enable different types of people to take leadership roles in the parish may subtly and unconsciously select favorites, those to whom they are attracted, those who excite them, for leadership positions. No wonder some clergy in long pastorates call the shots in their parishes. Our laity questionnaire asked for a sense of the major disadvantages of a long pastorate. Forty (twenty-eight percent) of the 144 responses centered around the following:

Loss of democratic decision making;
Pastor takes over--makes decisions;
Pastor picks favorites--less energy for others;
Loss of objectivity--pastor too involved in
personal relationships.

Thus the democratization of parish life is another area in long pastorates which needs vigilance and concern. What ways are there to ensure that all factions and viewpoints can continue to be expressed?

A Virginia congregation elects its vestry by lottery. The name of every baptised member of the parish is placed in a hat. At the annual meeting the parishioners whose names are the first four drawn are elected to the vestry for a three-year term. This is one way of ensuring that elections don't get skewed in one direction. What other ways are there for those in long pastorates to use to ensure such results?

Whatever method is chosen, underlying it must be a clergy/lay combination that, aware of the homogenization phenomenon, actively works to overcome it.

IV. Intervention Strategies

The Intervention Window

Other than praying that one of the three elements (effective crisis management, shared vision or life renewal) discussed in "Gap" prevention above will happen, how can healthy long pastorates be cultivated? There are ways in which judicatories can intervene to help pastorates move beyond the ten-year mark and have a good chance to be healthy, fruitful parishes.

We believe in every pastorate there exists a period, a "window," through which constructive intervention could be made. Beyond this period the pastorate will become a long one and intervention will become more difficult. The term "window," borrowed from NASA, refers to "space windows," the right times for shooting the moon or other extra terrestrial goals. Apollo launches must take place within these "windows" or be postponed for roughly a month. As in rocketry, the best interventions in the pastorate need to happen within certain parameters of time and dynamics. Some of the following criteria might characterize the "window:"

The time comes when the pastor knows that she/he has "been with" nearly every active parishioner through at least one personal crisis.

On a timeline, critical events in the congregation's life begin to diminish in frequency and "certain ways" of doing things begin to appear repeatedly. The more these recur, the less people think about them.

Lay leadership becomes more difficult to recruit. The same people begin to show up again and again; others experience lay burnout.

Feedback begins to become more difficult for laity to give and for the pastor to receive. Familiarity breeds reluctance to "level."

Individuals trust the pastor with confidential information as never before, or they say things such as "I'm so glad you are available," even if they seldom call on him/her.

The pastor and his/her family find their "roots" growing deep into the soil of the community. There is a real possibility of "going native," of losing the prophetic edge and sinking into the woodwork.

The time range is eight to twelve years into the pastorate. Even if none of the other criteria emerge, we think a significant intervention should be made well before the twelfth year.

It is our sense that this is a period of rich opportunity in a pastorate. But it is also a period that can pass too quickly and "staleness" sets in, or the "Gap" becomes such a powerful force that congregational health cannot be recovered. An intentional intervention by (or supported by) the judicatory in this "window" period can help pastor and parishioners address their life together.

What form should the intervention take? We cannot define all of its elements. Some components of the New England project might well be a part of such intervention. We suggest the following as part of intervention strategy:

Include the pastor and lay persons so both process and results can be commonly owned;

Use data from the history of the particular pastor/parish relationship;

Seek ways to test out the three elements discussed in "The Gap Theory" to gain a sense of whether these people feel these are part of their life;

Help people celebrate their story and feel "grace-filled" about their mutual life to date;

Give time, space and guidance to future planning for both parish and pastor.

If such an intervention can be well managed, it will inject "preventive" elements into the life of the parish: effective crisis management, shared vision and life renewal. We encourage intervention at the right time in the life of the pastorate. We anticipate many more creative long pastorates emerging if such interventions are made regularly and constructively.

We further suggest:

Board retreats focused on corporate congregational health;

Use of outside consultants;

Special task forces focused on the issue;

Pastor/parish relations committees paying more attention to the dangers of "Gap(s)."

Every pastorate is unique. Each has built into it certain strengths and certain liabilities, thus making it difficult to generalize about the problems of a long pastorate. Through this study, however, we have developed strong convictions about the need for clergy and laity involved in a long pastorate to test with each other the nature of the "Gap" that may be developing between them.

As clergy and laity begin to feel they fit like a comfortable old shoe, each will need the capacity to recontract for possibly painful yet growth producing ways of once again being partners in ministry.

In spite of the potential liabilities of a long term relationship between pastor and congregation, we remain convinced of the great potential advantage of long pastorates. Having identified some of the possible pitfalls, we would now like to address ways to keep long pastorates alive, vital and healthy. These recommendations grow out of the following convictions.

Long pastorates can either be a bane or a blessing. Much depends upon the skills and insight of both pastors and people in monitoring the relationship and advocating a corrective course when there are indications of a downward spiral.

Both pastor and parishioners often feel stuck in their ambivalence about their long pastorate. That ambivalence often has a depressing effect, as there appear to be few options for restoring pastoral vitality. This is partly because of the lack of benchmarks against which to measure a pastorate so that specific items can be addressed for improvement. It is our hope that the Support Pillars of Healthy Long Pastorates section will provide a set of such benchmarks against which clergy and congregations can measure and seek changes in the quality of their relationships.

Judicatory Support

As our work with long-term pastors unfolded, it became clear that participating in this decision-making process involved facing into heavy issues on the part of pastors and spouses.

When a pastor has invested ten or more years in a ministry, it is highly threatening to place that pastorate under a microscope for dissecting and analyzing. If the clergy are uncertain about whether or not they are currently "cutting the mustard," it is tempting for them to engage in avoidance and denial.

If clergy and spouses are to participate in a process that supports decision-making, whether they stay or leave, they will need support. Most appropriate is for middle judicatory personnel to suggest and support their clergy in their participation in seminars such as those sponsored by The Alban Institute. The middle judicatory has much to lose when clergy stuck in long pastorates fail either to revitalize those ministries or to move to other challenges.

Care needs to be exercised in the manner in which couples are asked to participate in these experiences. Suggested attendance should not imply: "It's time you moved on." This was how some couples in our first seminar perceived the bishop's invitation.

Middle judicatory officials can support clergy also by providing scholarships to help couples who wish to participate.

Conflict Management Skills

The Alban Institute study (specifically the first New England probe) revealed that the majority of the sixteen pastors studied had encountered and dealt effectively with serious conflicts with their congregations during the 1960s. Through the years, these pastors had drawn upon and refined skills learned in those difficult times.

Three basic generalizations emerged:

1. Where conflict is acknowledged and managed, congregational life is healthier. In a long pastorate pastoral care is a vital addition to conflict management skills;

2. Managing conflict is harder than managing organizational life. Long-tenured pastors tend to manage their organizational work better than their conflict, but both are crucial to long pastorate corporate health;

3. The most significant danger in the long pastorate is the absence of communication between pastor and laity. In congregations where conflict is avoided or buried, communication is vague, confused or misunderstood. People stop talking to one another except in the most polite or cautious terms.

In short, when tensions are avoided, conflict is suppressed, politeness reigns and everyone "loves" everyone else so much things get increasingly stale and boring.

Addressing Feelings of Abandonment

Clergy and their spouses are usually left alone to
determine the wisdom and health of either staying in
the same parish for another five to ten years or of
leaving. This abandonment results in ambivalence
with all its accompanying de-energizing factors.
Freedom, life and energy are either the cost of am-
bivalance or the promise of certainty. A participant
at the final evaluation said:

The greatest thing that happened to me was a con-
version experience. I came under protest, and
throughout both phases of the conference felt a
lifting of burden, anger, hostility and antagon-
ism, and these feelings were replaced with joy and
peace and a real sense that I am where God wants
me to be. It is a very spiritual experience. I
feel greatly affirmed by the group as far as our
decision to stay is concerned. It is very reas-
suring to have the group say to my spouse what I
have said and felt previously. I am encouraged
and eager to face what lies ahead for us in the
parish. There is so much life there, and I have
the feeling that the Spirit is moving within the
parish and within us as well. The next few years
appear full of promise, and I have nowhere to go
but up. I am a new person--spiritually as well as
emotionally.

The gratitude the research team received from the
participants is rewarding. It is also indicative of
the necessity to assist clergy and spouses in long
pastorates to resolve their ambivalence and get on
with life--either in a new parish or in their current
one.

Clergy Risk

For clergy to remain healthy and human in long pastorates, a favorable climate needs to exist for them
to take risks in three areas:

Risk accepting their fears so they are able to
grow;

Risk having parishioners become aware that, even
though clergy demonstrate competence, they still have
need for grace;
　　Risk facing their fear of failure.
When the climate in the congregation is not supportive enough for clergy to take these three risks, or
when clergy themselves are too frightened to risk in
spite of a supportive climate, the long pastorate
will be negatively affected.

Risking Growth
Growth involves moving into areas of fear and vulner-
ability. The growing edge is the place where one is
most uptight and frightened. When clergy fail to
move into their areas of fear, they get stuck and
settle for the status quo. This is most acutely felt
over time in a long pastorate.

Risking Grace
Clergy need to demonstrate their competence in parish
life. If, however, they demonstrate only competence,
they fail to illustrate the grace they preach to
others. Their explicit theology proclaims grace;
their operational theology proclaims omnipotence.
Parishioners listen to and model themselves after the
theology proclaimed in the way their ministers live.
Unless clergy are able to risk demonstrating how
grace works in their lives, they end up giving a
double message. Long pastorates are most affected by
such double talk.

Risking Failure
Most of us cover our fear of failure with frantic
activity and hard work. Our fear of failure,
however, is what prevents us from letting go and
envisioning new possibilities. It prevents us from
letting go of old approaches and methods. Even when
we know things aren't working well, we accept that at
least they aren't complete failures. We'd rather go
with a partial success than risk complete failure.
But, when we are willing to risk failure, we give
ourselves and others room to test new ideas and

approaches.   In a long pastorate this is an important
commodity.

A nonsupportive and threatening parish climate
prevents clergy from risking on any of these three
levels, creating a standoff, issuing in nonproductive
interaction between pastor and parish.   In the long
haul it spells death for both.

V. Reflections

The Seminars

If you have followed these research results and
learnings to this point, and still feel a need for
more help in coming to terms with your long pastorate, we would recommend that you seek out a
cosponsored Alban Institute/local judicatory seminar
on this issue. We are only too aware of our inability to encapsulate in writing the experiences we
have had with clergy and their spouses in our Long-
Tenured Pastorate Seminars. Even though our primary
task was that of discovering more about long pastorates, we are aware that we were also of significant
help to those who attended.

It's difficult to identify exactly what seminar
ingredients led to powerful change in the lives of
the participants. Was it the readiness of the couples who attended? Was it the deep trust that developed in these "safe" ecumenical settings? Was it the
openness and caring of the staff, that helped participants regain a sense of confidence and stability?
Was it the design that got at issues rarely addressed
by the church? No doubt, it was a combination of
some or all of these. At each closing Eucharist,
however, we were all aware of the concrete way in
which the Spirit had been present with us. A brief
example illustrates the nature of the changes that
occurred.

Bill and Ellen Manrodt came to Phase I of the
second New England seminar fairly certain they wanted
to continue their ministry in Massachusetts. Bill
had been rector there for ten years. He and Ellen
had been married only five years, so Ellen was not a

"long-tenured spouse." An ordained priest herself, Ellen's career as a pastoral counselor was just beginning to take hold. Her private practice as a therapist was also growing substantially. Both were very attached to the people in the parish as well as the community.

With the decision to stay as a given, we began to assist them to be in touch with the issues that need attention when one stays in one place over a prolonged period. The "Gap" theory made a deep impression on Bill. He began to work out ways to prevent "Gaps" occuring in his parish. We also began to press the couple about what new vision they had for the next five years.

When they returned for the Phase II seminar, it was obvious that Bill was depressed. During the session on stress and burnout, Bill's burnout score was thirty-eight. A score of twenty-five to thirty-six is considered serious. If he were to stay, what did he need to do for himself to prevent complete burnout? Bill confessed his boredom with his parish, but he continually refused to consider moving for two reasons: his love for the people in his parish and Ellen's career needs.

Ellen was licensed as a therapist in Massachusetts, a credential not readily transferable to other states, and required for collecting insurance fees from clients. Her D. Min. in Pastoral Counseling might not be recognized by other states.

In the midst of a small group discussion focused on Bill's depression and burnout, Ellen burst into tears. She had been watching Bill's depression for months. She felt helpless not knowing what to do. She had hoped the depression would subside, but it hadn't. Out of concern for him and their marriage, she advocated his moving to another job. (See Instrument Section.) She had said as much before, but Bill had not believed her. The straightforward questioning of the group facilitator broke through their miscommunication. From that point onward both of them began to work at the other end of the stay/-leave continuum. (See Instrument Section.) Together

they decided that either way it was going to be painful for them, but moving seemed to offer more promise
of regaining their health and happiness.

In a followup telephone conversation with Bill ten
months later, he indicated that he had had ten in-
quiries. The couple was still clear that moving
would be best. Bill also reported some exciting
things happening to him in his present parish. A
real parish spiritual awakening seemed to be occur-
ring. Bill attributed it to his internal spiritual
awakening going on as a result of both the LTP seminar and several other events he had chosen to be
part of since. "At this point," Bill reports, "It's
going to be a new future for us, whether we stay or
leave; but we are still pressing for a call elsewhere."

This is but one example of the kinds of dramatic
changes we witnessed in the lives of participants.
Some of the people who came found themselves really
stuck. We believe we were able to help them begin to
get some movement into their lives again. Others who
came were in a good deal of pain. The individualized
help and support we were able to give them left many
feeling comforted, feeling they had some handles on
how to address their pain. A major contributor to
the risking and the succeeding was the kind of supportive community that developed in each of the three
groups. We spent good chunks of time on team building at the beginning of each seminar. We perceived
that a nurturing community was essential for the
kinds of risks we would be asking people to take as
they assessed their pastorates and planned for the
future.

Another important factor in the positive outcome
of our seminars was the inclusion of spouses in the
entire experience. More than once we heard these
women saying, "This is the first time the church has
said clearly that it values me and my perspective."
We will argue long and hard for the inclusion of
spouses in long pastorate seminars. It is simply un-
fair and irresponsible to ask clergy to carry out a
major assessment of their ministry, to develop future

plans and then to return home and lay these conclu-
sions on their spouses. The spouses' future is intimately integrated with the clergy's future. We do
not see how a seminar could proceed with only one of
them present.

Two other aspects of our design stand out as
important for us:

1. We separated the two week seminars by a three
month period for data gathering, dialogue, and reflection. In each case when people returned for
Phase II of the experience we could tell that much
movement had occurred in their lives. For many,
dramatic changes in life direction only occur when
plenty of time and space is available.

2. We developed a stay/leave continuum that
proved to be very effective in helping people identify where they were in relation to their pastorate.
This seemed to be a necessary first step in assisting
them to move towards a more definite stance. The
continuum consisted of six definite stances toward
their pastorate ranging from stance one (I'm clear
about staying; I want to work on a new vision and a
fresh start where I am) to stance six (I'm clear
about moving; I need to get my act together so I can
facilitate a move for myself).

We continued to affirm people who took a stand at
either end, and we were prepared to work in depth
with them. It is just as important to make specific
plans for how staying in the parish is going to be
challenging, productive, and health producing, as it
is to make plans for moving.

At the beginning of each seminar, however, the
majority of participants were stuck in the middle of
the continuum at stances two through five. We
strongly believed that to be stuck in the ambivalence
of stances two through five was energy draining. We
were quite open about our intention to move participants to either stance one or six by the end of the
second seminar. Much of our time was spent in helping them identify the causes of their ambivalence so

they could become clearer about moving to a definite "stay" or a definite "leave." This sometimes involved encouraging participants to gather specific data in their parish between the two seminars. Other help included value clarification designs we developed. We demanded a lot from these participants, and in the end they indicated their appreciation for the demands. Approximately one third of those attending the three seminars ended with a definite commitment to move to a new situation within a year. The remaining two-thirds worked on how, now that they had made a definite commitment to stay, they would build new life and energy into their continued work in their parish.

Goals and Objectives

Goal

To increase the effectiveness and quality of one's ministry through a more informed and intentional decision-making process on the part of clergy and spouses in a long pastorate.

Objectives

To engage in disciplined reflection on our long pastorate through the use of various theories and hypotheses;

To study and integrate feedback from our parish and laity related to the long pastorate;

To engage in personal reflections on our ministry through the use of a variety of instruments: The Stay/Leave Continuum, The Pastor/Parish Fit Instrument, The Myers-Briggs Type Indicator, Burnout Rating Scales, The Strain Response Inventory;

Through discussion, reflection and planning to outline personal and professional goals for the next five years.

Additional Reflections

In addition, there were findings on the use of action research intervention with this population:

The seminar responded to a participant need not being addressed elsewhere in the church system, reaching pastors existentially where their fears and doubts were most active;

The participants came with an attitude of readiness to explore and change rather than with the intransigence anticipated by the researchers;

The support of the denominational executives and the message conveyed by the way in which they invited participants to attend the seminar was crucial to the attitude of participants and their willingness to explore their LTP;

The design valued the spouse's contribution and perspective as the clergy made a major assessment of their ministry;

The inclusion of spouses was imperative to the success of the intervention;

The interaction of sharing with and supporting each other throughout the experience was significantly valued by the participants, and identified as not being readily available "back home;"

A "safe" ecumenical mix of both participants and researchers helped create trust among the participants;

Significant movement occurred in the participants during the lengthy interim period of time and space for data gathering, dialogue, and reflection;

The Pastor/Parish Fit was an effective instrument in assisting clergy who have been left to their own resources to ascertain their current "fit" with their congregations in determining that fit;

The responsiveness of the researchers and the emerging design allowed the participants to trust and invest themselves in the seminar;

The open and caring styles of the researchers created a sense of confidence and stability for the participants;

There appear to be clergy whose personality type and skills are particularly suited for a LTP;

A compilation of the thoughtful laity response was an indication of their investment in the quality of the pastorate and valuable to interpretation and discussion in the design;

Participants were openly frustrated by some written data gathering during the seminars, yet acknowledged their understanding of its importance for research purposes;

Elements of the design were evaluated by various participants as least useful when task directions were not clear, when resistance was present or when the task was not completed at all.

Because of scheduling conflicts the three researchers were male during the first phases of the pilot seminar--an imbalance inconsistent with the values and wishes of the project designers, and the subsequent addition of one or two women (who were also LTP spouses) to the team was positively acknowledged by participants and others;

The seminars enabled clergy and spouses in LTP to explore their present situation extensively and from various perspectives and to begin to determine what direction was best both for them and for the congregations they served;

In particular, a stay/leave continuum and related
parts of the seminar design enabled participants to
move from being tentative and ambivalent regarding
their present situation to making a clear and
definite commitment to stay or leave. All of the
sixty-six participants came to the seminar with some
doubts and questions about staying in their current
positions, yet only two remained ambivalent regarding
their direction at the conclusion of the seminar.
Thus, the design achieved the intended outcome of
assisting participants to clarify their attitudes
toward both their LTP and their future direction.

Summary

For the present, it's enough for us as a team
heartily to affirm long pastorates and to invite
those engaged in them to work hard to overcome
potential disadvantages. In no way, however, do we
imply this is easy work. It requires vigilance,
skill and, occasionally, the use of outside resources. In many ways, maintaining a healthy long
pastorate is more difficult than changing pastorates
every five to eight years. Clergy can dazzle and
even fool a congregation over shorter periods of
ministry. Many simply repeat their five year bag of
tricks everywhere they go. In a long pastorate,
people get to know their clergy very well, both their
assets and their liabilities. These clergy either
need to be genuine, authentic persons who live by
what they preach and advocate or, to the detriment of
their ministry, they are soon found out. It is infi-
nitely easier to be the spiritual mentor of people
over the short haul than over the long haul. In a
long pastorate, clergy soon exhaust whatever wisdom
or knowledge they brought to the scene and must continue to scramble to grow personally or end up re-
peating themselves and boring others. But those who
do grow, who do monitor the other disadvantages of a
long pastorate, will be likely to have a ministry
that is very rewarding and fulfilling. They can
experience a closeness and intimacy with people that

comes only with time. Their pastoral interventions
can have the perspective of experience and knowledge
of people. They know their people, how far they have
stretched and grown and how much further they can be
challenged to greater spiritual maturity. They are
aware of a parish's growth potential and know when to
press for new spurts of development. Their sense of
timing is keener than those in shorter pastorates.
We hope those of you in these long pastorates sense
these advantages and press on to confront the things
that, given their natural course, are likely to go
wrong in your long pastorate.

We continue to be impressed with the fact that all
the disadvantages or hazards of a long pastorate are
surmountable, yet few of the advantages of a long
pastorate are available to clergy present in a parish
for only a short period of time. There are so many
advantages to long pastorates that struggling with
their hazards or pitfalls is well worth while.

Robert Schuller of the Church Growth Institute in
California has observed that few congregations experience major spurts in growth until the pastor has
been there for a minimum of five to eight years.
Most significant growth happens when a pastor has
been in place at least ten years. It takes time for
clergy to gain the kind of credibility, trust and
knowledge necessary for such major growth. This includes credibility and respect within the community
as well as the parish.

In a period when stress and instability are the
daily reality of people's lives, how fortunate many
of them are to have a long-time trusted and caring
friend in their parish pastor. Today, when people
are so mobile, we need clergy who are models of
stability. Clergy can become the anchor that keeps
people grounded in reality, especially the reality of
God's grace for their lives.

Contributors

This project consisted of three separate study
groups, involving thirty-four clergy and twenty-six
spouses. Each study group met for two four-day seminars with a three month field work project in the
interim between the seminars.

The completion of this study project and the
writing of this monograph has been the collaborative
effort of four people.

ROY M. OSWALD, Project Coordinator, was involved
in all three research probes and was final editor of
this monograph.

BARTON M. LLOYD was in on this project from the
beginning, and with Roy and Loren Mead first defined
the need and outlined the project. Bart brought the
resources of the New England Career Center to the
project.

WILLIAM CHRIS HOBGOOD, who has just completed a
Doctor of Ministry degree at Lancaster Theological
Seminary, was also in on the project from the
beginning. He brought both his knowledge from his
dissertation, "The Long-Tenured Pastor"[5] and his
personal experience as a long-tenured pastor to the
project.

GAIL D. HINAND, Doctoral candidate at Boston
University,[6] contributed greatly with both her
experience as a long-tenured pastorate spouse and her
expertise as a trainer, consultant and therapist.

Due to budget constraints, Bart was not involved
in the North Carolina study and Chris was not in-
volved in the second New England study. In North
Carolina, we utilized the skills and services of RUTH
WRIGHT, free lance trainer and consultant for the
Diocese of North Carolina.

Appendix: Instruments

Myers-Briggs Type Indicator

Many are familiar with the categories of the M.B.T.I.
The survey measures people's preference for either

    Extroversion - Introversion
    Sensing   - iNtuition
    Thinking   - Feeling
    Judging   - Perceiving

People who take the indicator emerge with four
letters, i.e., INFP or ESTJ, which communicate their
type. The combination of letters or preferences
indicate important differences between people.

Stay/Leave Continuum

1. I am definitely going to stay. I need to become
clearer now about the goals and vision that will
sustain my energy for the next five years.

2. I am going to stay, but there are some things I
need to resolve before making that a definite "yes."

3. I am committed to staying in this parish right
now, but a part of me is uneasy about that decision.
I need to discover the source of my uneasiness.

4. My inclination is to begin looking for a move,
although there is still a lot that is here beckoning
me to stay longer.

5. It feels best that I begin the process of finding a call elsewhere. I need to discover what is holding me back from doing that with greater energy.

6. I'm definitely going to move. I need to get my act together and find the next challenge to match my talents and interests.

The Pastor/Parish Fit

A special instrument was developed for our Long Pastorate study to assist clergy to measure the current "fit" between them and their congregations. Since the pastor/parish dynamic constantly shifts, what was once congenial may no longer be. Over time both clergy and congregation change. What was once experienced as a challenge by clergy may no longer seem to be one. Congregations may outgrow their clergy, demanding more from them than they are capable of producing. Interest or investment in different types of ministry may also separate clergy and their congregations. Laity may want one type of ministry, while their clergy feel they have "other fish to fry."

Clergy in long pastorates have been, by and large, left to their own resources to figure out the state of their pastor/parish fit, whether or not it felt right anymore. It is hoped that this instrument will help clergy to clarify any areas in which there is no clear fit between themselves and their parish and will give them an overall picture of their pastor/parish fit.

For the statements listed below, please indicate your response by checking one of the answer categories. This instrument measures not only the levels of compatibility/incompatibility you experience with your parish, but also areas of your work which for you are most tension laden. In each question, read sections A. and B. together, exploring the extent to which there is tension between these two in your ministry. Record the extent of that tension by the appropriate number differences between A. and B. Where you experience no tension, both A. and B. should receive the same number score.

For each question choose the best description and place a check in the box below the appropriate number.

1. A. You are required to work to full capacity.

   B. You would like to be required to work to full capacity.

2. A. Excellence is required of you.

   B. You would like excellence to be required of you.

3. A. You have a responsibility for the work of others.
   B. You would like responsibility for the work of Others.

4. A. You have responsibility for budgets and expenditures.
   B. You would like responsibility for budgets and expenditures.

5. A. Your role as pastor is defined.

   B. You would like your role as pastor defined.

6. A. You work face-to-face with individual parishioners.
   B. You would like to work face-to-face with individual parishioners.

7. A. You have say or influence over how your congregation is run.
   B. You would like to have say or influence over how your congregation is run.

Rarely Very few Very little 1	Seldom Few Little 2	Sometimes Some Some 3	Often Many Much 4	Very Often Many Much 5
☐	☐	☐	☐	☐
☐	☐	☐	☐	☐
☐	☐	☐	☐	☐
☐	☐	☐	☐	☐
☐	☐	☐	☐	☐
☐	☐	☐	☐	☐
☐	☐	☐	☐	☐
☐	☐	☐	☐	☐
☐	☐	☐	☐	☐
☐	☐	☐	☐	☐
☐	☐	☐	☐	☐
☐	☐	☐	☐	☐
☐	☐	☐	☐	☐
☐	☐	☐	☐	☐

8. A. Your governing board delegates responsibility to you and supports you in the same.
   B. You would like your governing board to delegate responsibility and support you in the same.

9. A. Fellow clergy are helpful and supportive.

   B. You would like fellow clergy to be helpful and supportive.

10. A. You have the trust and confidence of your staff.
    B. You would like to have the trust and confidence of your staff.

11. A. Data is available to you to determine the effectiveness of your ministry.
    B. You would like data to be available to you to assess your ministry.

12. A. The environment in which you live and work is a source of joy and pleasure.
    B. You would like your environment to be a source of joy and pleasure.

13. A. You have a sense of job security and overall well-being in your current parish.
    B. You would like to have a sense of job security and well-being.

14. A. The growth and development of your parish is a source of satisfaction.
    B. You would like the growth and development of the parish to be a source of satisfaction.

Rarely Very few Very little 1	Seldom Few Little 2	Sometimes Some Some 3	Often Many Much 4	Very Often Many Much 5
☐	☐	☐	☐	☐
☐	☐	☐	☐	☐
☐	☐	☐	☐	☐
☐	☐	☐	☐	☐
☐	☐	☐	☐	☐
☐	☐	☐	☐	☐
☐	☐	☐	☐	☐
☐	☐	☐	☐	☐
☐	☐	☐	☐	☐
☐	☐	☐	☐	☐
☐	☐	☐	☐	☐
☐	☐	☐	☐	☐
☐	☐	☐	☐	☐
☐	☐	☐	☐	☐

15. A. This parish continually pushes you onto your growing edge.
    B. You would like your parish to challenge and stimulate you.

16. A. You like your parishioners and they like you.

    B. You would like to like your parishioners and have them like you.

17. A. You are expected to complete a large quantity of work.
    B. You would like to be expected to complete a large quantity of work.

18. A. Your current parish ministry challenges you.

    B. You would like to have challenge in your parish ministry.

19. A. You are required to supervise the work of others.
    B. You would like to be required to supervise the work of others.

20. A. You have responsibility for equipment and maintenance of facilities.
    B. You would like to have responsibility for equipment and maintenance of facilities.

21. A. Parish priorities are made clear to you.

    B. You would like parish priorities to be made clear for you.

Rarely Very few Very little 1	Seldom Few Little 2	Sometimes Some Some 3	Often Many Much 4	Very Often Many Much 5
☐	☐	☐	☐	☐
☐	☐	☐	☐	☐
☐	☐	☐	☐	☐
☐	☐	☐	☐	☐
☐	☐	☐	☐	☐
☐	☐	☐	☐	☐
☐	☐	☐	☐	☐
☐	☐	☐	☐	☐
☐	☐	☐	☐	☐
☐	☐	☐	☐	☐
☐	☐	☐	☐	☐
☐	☐	☐	☐	☐
☐	☐	☐	☐	☐
☐	☐	☐	☐	☐

22. A. Your performance is dependent on the work of committees and boards.
    B. You would like your performance to be dependent on the work of committees and boards.

23. A. You have to carry out your responsibilities.

    B. You would like to have to carry out your responsibilities.

24. A. You trust your governing board and have confidence in their decisions.
    B. You'd like to be able to trust and have confidence in your governing board's decisions.

25. A. Persons in your clergy group/association are helpful and supportive of one another.
    B. You would like persons in your clergy group/-association to be helpful and supportive of each other.

26. A. Your staff works together as a cohesive team.

    B. You would like your staff to work together as a cohesive team.

27. A. People let you know when your work is appreciated.
    B. You would like people to let you know when they appreciate your work.

28. A. The parishioners with whom you work have similar values, tastes, and life styles to yours.
    B. You would like your parishioners to have similar values, tastes and life styles to yours.

Rarely Very few Very little 1	Seldom Few Little 2	Sometimes Some Some 3	Often Many Much 4	Very Often Many Much 5
☐	☐	☐	☐	☐
☐	☐	☐	☐	☐
☐	☐	☐	☐	☐
☐	☐	☐	☐	☐
☐	☐	☐	☐	☐
☐	☐	☐	☐	☐
☐	☐	☐	☐	☐
☐	☐	☐	☐	☐
☐	☐	☐	☐	☐
☐	☐	☐	☐	☐
☐	☐	☐	☐	☐
☐	☐	☐	☐	☐
☐	☐	☐	☐	☐
☐	☐	☐	☐	☐

29. A. Your career path is being enhanced by your present ministry.
    B. You would like your career path to be enhanced by your present ministry.

30. A. The governing board is satisfied with the growth of this parish.
    B. You would like your governing board to be satisfied with the growth of the parish.

31. A. There is support in the parish for you to engage in annual continuing education events.
    B. You would like the support of the parish for annual growth events.

32. A. There is tension between you and the parish.

    B. You would like for there to be tension between you and the parish.

Rarely	Seldom	Sometimes	Often	Very Often
Very few	Few	Some	Many	Many
Very little	Little	Some	Much	Much
1	2	3	4	5

☐   ☐   ☐   ☐   ☐
☐   ☐   ☐   ☐   ☐

☐   ☐   ☐   ☐   ☐
☐   ☐   ☐   ☐   ☐

☐   ☐   ☐   ☐   ☐
☐   ☐   ☐   ☐   ☐

☐   ☐   ☐   ☐   ☐
☐   ☐   ☐   ☐   ☐

Summary

Step A: The score for each number box should reflect the difference in your answer between questions A. and B. For example:

A.
☐ ☐ [X] ☐ ☐   Difference: 2

B.
☐ ☐ ☐ ☐ [X]

OR:

A.
☐ ☐ ☐ [X] ☐   Difference: 0

B.
☐ ☐ ☐ [X] ☐

Return to your answer sheets and record all the differences between answers A. and B. in the boxes on this tally sheet below.

<u>Step B</u>: Add numbers in boxes next to each other for category score.

1. ☐ + 17. ☐ = ☐ Quantitative Workload

2. ☐ + 18. ☐ = ☐ Qualitative Workload

3. ☐ + 19. ☐ = ☐ Responsibility for Persons

4. ☐ + 20. ☐ = ☐ Responsibility for Things

5. ☐ + 21. ☐ = ☐ Role Ambiguity

6. ☐ + 22. ☐ = ☐ Interfacing

7. ☐ + 23. ☐ = ☐ Authority/ Influence

8. ☐ + 24. ☐ = ☐ Board Relations

9. ☐ + 25. ☐ = ☐ Peer Relations

10. ☐ + 26. ☐ = ☐ Subordinate Relations

11. ☐ + 27. ☐ = ☐ Feedback

12. □ + 28. □ = □ Personal & Physical Work Environment

---

13. □ + 29. □ = □ Job Security/Career Satisfaction

---

14. □ + 30. □ = □ Congregational Growth and Development

15. □ + 31. □ = □ Personal/Professional Development

---

16. □ + 32. □ = □ Trust/Compatibility

Step C: Now total the numbers in the right hand column.

Interpretation

Total Scores

1 - 16   There is reasonable to high compatibility between you and this parish.

17 - 30   Tension and dissatisfaction between you and this parish are mounting.

31 - on   There is a high degree of incompatibility between you and this parish.

Burnout Rating and Strain Response Scales

Burnout Rating Scale

The following Burnout Rating Scale was utilized with participants in our last two study groups. Both scores and participation in the seminars revealed that one out of every four clergy in those groups was bordering on burnout, one out of six was clearly in the burnout state, and one out of ten was an extreme case of burnout.

To use this scale, circle the rating that most applies in each of the nine burnout categories. Then total the numbers circled.

1. The extent to which I am feeling negative or cynical about the parishioners with whom I work, despairing of their ability to change and grow

1	2	3	4	5	6

Optimistic about
clients

Cynical about
clients

2. The extent to which I have enthusiasm for parish ministry, enjoy my work and look forward to it regularly

1	2	3	4	5	6

High internal energy
for my work

Loss of enthu-
siasm for my job

3. The extent to which I invest myself emotionally in my ministry and in parishioners

1	2	3	4	5	6

High emotional
investment

Withdrawal and
emotional de-
tachment

4. The extent to which fatigue and irritation are part of my daily experience

1	2	3	4	5	6

Cheerfulness, high
energy much of the time

Fatigue and irri-
tation much of
the time

5. The extent to which my humor has a cynical, biting tone to it

1	2	3	4	5	6

Humor reflecting a positive,
joyful attitude

Cynical and
sarcastic humor

6. The extent to which I find myself spending less and less time with my parishioners

1	2	3	4	5	6

Normal and anticipated
contact with clients

Increased with-
drawal from
clients

7. The extent to which I am becoming less flexible in my dealings with parishioners

1	2	3	4	5	6

Openness and flexibility
to client's needs and wants

Rigidity in
dealing with
clients

8. The extent to which I feel supported in my ministry

1	2	3	4	5	6

Feeling of
full support

Feeling of
isolation

9. The extent to which I find myself frustrated in my attempts to accomplish tasks

1	2	3	4	5	6

Tasks important to me
normally completed

Tasks important
to me frequent-
ly thwarted

_____Total of numbers circled.

Analysis of Burnout Survey Scores

0 - 18   Positive and healthy attitudes towards
          self, others and ministry.

19 - 25   Borderline burnout. Care should be
          taken that burnout does not become more
          of a factor in your life and ministry.

25 - 36   Burnout a factor in your life. It's important to set into motion self-care practices that will reverse this process.

36 +   Extreme burnout a reality in your life. More radical self-care practices needed to reverse this process. Reaching out for help and assistance advised.

To ascertain the effects of your current state of burnout, the following strain response scale may be helpful. It points up and measures the ways in which your burnout manifests itself in certain dysfunctional aspects of life.

Typical Strain Responses to Burnout

Our natural physical and psychological response to burnout is referred to as strain. The twenty-four items below are examples of strain responses. That is, when we are experiencing burnout it is likely that we will respond as described by one or more of these items.

This instrument is designed to help you become more aware of your strain response patterns. It is not a complete list by any means, but should provide a point of departure for further investigations.

Please assign a value to each item according to how often it is true of your behavior or feelings as follows:

0 = Never
1 = Infrequently
2 = Frequently
3 = Regularly

_____ 1. Eat too much
_____ 2. Drink too much alcohol
_____ 3. Smoke more than usual
_____ 4. Feel tense, uptight, fidgety
_____ 5. Feel depressed or remorseful

_____ 6. Like myself less
_____ 7. Have difficulty going to sleep or
           staying asleep
_____ 8. Feel restless and unable to concen-
           trate
_____ 9. Have decreased interest in sex
_____ 10. Have increased interest in sex
_____ 11. Have loss of appetite
_____ 12. Feel tired/low energy
_____ 13. Feel irritable
_____ 14. Think about suicide
_____ 15. Become less communicative
_____ 16. Feel disoriented or overwhelmed
_____ 17. Have difficulty getting up in the
           morning
_____ 18. Have headaches
_____ 19. Have upset stomach
_____ 20. Have sweaty and/or trembling hands
_____ 21. Have shortness of breath and sighing
_____ 22. Let things slide
_____ 23. Misdirect anger
_____ 24. Feel "unhealthy"

TOTAL SCORE

Analysis of Strain Response Scale

0 - 20   Below average strain in your life.
21 - 28   The strain of life and work is begin-
            ing to show its effects.
29 - 35   Above average strain. Burnout is hav-
            ing a very distructive effect on your
            life.
36 +   Unless you do something to alleviate
            the stress and burnout of your life,
            more serious illness is likely to-
            follow.

108

Footnotes

1. William Douglas, <u>Ministers' Wives</u> (Harper & Rowe, 1965).

2. It bears remarking that our research into every aspect of ministry continues to turn up areas in which widely held notions are found to be quite wrong. The bits of "common knowledge" and "good advice" that often influence what actually happens are usually unexamined and frequently not based on fact.

3. Daniel J. Levinson, <u>The Seasons of a Man's Life</u>, (Ballantine, Random House, 1978).

4. James R. Adams and Celia A. Hahn, <u>Learning to Share the Ministry</u>, (Alban Institute, 1975).

5. William Chris Hobgood, <u>The Long-Tenured Pastorate: A Study of Ways to Build Trust.</u> Unpublished doctoral dissertation, (Lancaster Theological Seminary, 1982).

6. Gail D. Hinand, <u>Action research as a preventative intervention model: A study of the Long-Tenured Pastorate</u>, a comprehensive treatise in partial fulfillment of requirements for Doctor of Education in Counseling Psychology, Boston University, 1982.

The Alban Institute:
an invitation to membership

The Alban Institute, begun in 1979, believes that the congregation is essential to the task of equipping the people of God to minister in the church and the world. A multi-denominational membership organization, the Institute provides on-site training, educational programs, consulting, research, and publishing for hundreds of churches across the country.

The Alban Institute invites you to be a member of this partnership of laity, clergy, and executives—a partnership that brings together people who are raising important questions about congregational life and people who are trying new solutions, making new discoveries, finding a new way of getting clear about the task of ministry. The Institute exists to provide you with the kinds of information and resources you need to support your ministries.

Join us now and enjoy these benefits:

CONGREGATIONS, The Alban Journal, a highly respected journal published six times a year, to keep you up to date on current issues and trends.

Inside Information, Alban's quarterly newsletter, keeps you informed about research and other happenings around Alban. Available to members only.

Publications Discounts:

☐ 15% for Individual, Retired Clergy, and Seminarian Members
☐ 25% for Congregational Members
☐ 40% for Judicatory and Seminary Executive Members

Discounts on Training and Education Events

Write our Membership Department at the address below or call us at 1-800-718-4407 or 301-718-4407 for more information about how to join The Alban Institute's growing membership, particularly about Congregational Membership in which 12 designated persons receive all benefits of membership.

The Alban Institute, Inc.
Suite 433 North
4550 Montgomery Avenue
Bethesda, MD 20814-3341